FAMILIES CAN BOUNCE BACK

FAMILIES CAN BOUNCE BACK

— COMPILED BY —

DIANA L. JAMES

HORIZON BOOKS

CAMP HILL, PENNSYLVANIA

HORIZON BOOKS

A DIVISION OF CHRISTIAN PUBLICATIONS, INC.
3825 Hartzdale Drive, Camp Hill, PA 17011
www.cpi-horizon.com
www.christianpublications.com

ISBN: 0-88965-194-9
LOC Control Number: 01-130447
© 2001 by Horizon Books
All rights reserved
Printed in the United States of America

01 02 03 04 05   5 4 3 2 1

Lovingly dedicated to each
and every member of my
three fantastic families:
biological, step and extended.
I believe in you!
I love you all!

ZIGGY ©1998 ZIGGY AND FRIENDS, INC.
Reprinted with permission of UNIVERSAL PRESS
SYNDICATE. All rights reserved.

Contents

Acknowledgments

My deepest appreciation to all the
wonderful people who so
generously contributed these
stories of triumph and faith.
Heartfelt thanks to my husband, Max,
whose special talents, tireless help
and encouragement blessed me in
the preparation of this book.

Introduction

This book is the fourth in my "Bounce Back" series, having been preceded by *Bounce Back*, *You Can Bounce Back Too* and *Teens Can Bounce Back*. Like its forerunners, *Families Can Bounce Back* offers an inspiring potpourri of true experiences and stories of significance, perhaps with a touch of humor but always with the promise of spiritual help.

In this book, I present testimonies of faith that may inspire a renewal of the bonds of love among family members. If there is any trace of resentment, bitterness, disappointment, emotional pain, loneliness or fear, I pray that one of these stories will bring the reader a bright ray of hope and a deeper faith in God's healing power, limitless love, caring and grace.

The selections are divided into six sections, representing relationships within the family unit. Some people long to feel and express the love that binds people together in the unique kinship of a family. Some may have lost or never have known the warmth of family affection and loyalty that goes deeper than friendship. Each of the stories you are about to read can offer you an "ah-ha" realization or a nugget of inspiration. I pray with confidence that this book will find its way into the hands of those who need, and

1

are ready to receive, these messages of encouragement.

May the Lord bless you. May you grow in your faith. May your family abound in love and abide in Him from whom all blessings flow.

—DLJ

Section 1

Families

Choose for yourselves this day whom you will serve. . . . But as for me and my household, we will serve the LORD.
(Joshua 24:15)

Home and Family in Kenya

Vincent Muli Wa Kituku

You can live with less if you have something to live for. Quality of life is not the abundance of material possessions, state-of-the-art gadgets and an unlimited supply of modern conveniences. These are useful, but I lacked them all when I was growing up in Kenya, and I missed nothing.

The house most vivid in my memory was built in 1965. I shared this somewhat rectangular two bedroom, one-living room structure with my parents and three siblings. Over time, four other siblings were born there, so to create space for the new arrivals and provide my sister some privacy, my brother and I used the living room as our bedroom.

Our family shared this habitat with other species. Rats would scurry for cover the moment someone entered an empty room. When their numbers were no longer bearable, my mother would schedule "rat reduction day." This was always an event to remember. One of us would pour hot water into one end of the rat holes while the other waited with militant readiness at the other end with the sole mission of killing as many rats as they could as the vermin ran from the hot water.

Our home was also the residence for rat predators—snakes and rat ticks. We kept our drinking water in a clay pot positioned in one corner of the living room. This corner served as a cool haven for snakes as they waited patiently for their prey. Sometimes, when there was little water in the pot and one had to tilt it in order to scoop water with a calabash or cup, a snake would poke up its head looking for whoever was in its territory.

The presence of a snake brought everything else to a standstill. It had to be eliminated. One snake dared to crawl over my mother's legs when she was on her knees praying. When it finally left her, she called me; but she had taken care of the snake with a rock by the time I arrived.

Ticks seemed less dangerous and were fairly easy to combat. My brother, Kisingu, had only one job: to pour water on the floor and thus make it harder for the ticks to jump. (Now, I'm somewhat of an environmentalist and would be the last person to advocate unwarranted destruction of environmental resources in the chain of life, but in this case it was a matter of survival.)

It was in this home that I learned the adage, *You can live with less if you have something to live for.* Hard work and school were top priorities in our home. My hardworking father set up a small shop selling clothes, food stuffs and other items Kangundo folks would buy. He frequently admonished us about the importance of education and demanded that we be reading when he came home at night.

My mother brought another dimension—faith and folk tales—to our lives. She modeled for us a deep faith in God, praying before bedtime, meals and work. She sang church songs. The Easter ones were my favorites. At times, she told me folk tales as we were cultivating or cooking. Often she would concentrate on school-related lessons. One day, while fertilizing our garden with composted manure, my mother taught me the secret of solving multiplication problems.

The structure that we called our house was unstable and needed constant remodeling. However, the more important amenities—love for children, encouragement, hope for a better tomorrow, hard work and the knowledge of the existence of God—were not lacking. Rats, snakes, ticks, lack of shoes or sometimes missing a meal here and there were never considered long-term problems.

By 1979, the year I dismantled the original structure of our home (which by then served as a kitchen), Dad had realized his dream of a better future in the form of a fenced compound with nine bedrooms, a water fountain and two sons in higher institutes of learning. Dad is a living example of what vision, determination and hard work can accomplish irrespective of the dismal resources available.

My mother is a devout Christian. Her God became my God on March 9, 1985 when I gave my life to Jesus Christ. She is also a walking treasury of folklore. In 1996 (now living in America), I transcribed the oral folk tales she shared with me into the book, *East African Folk Tales for All Ages from the Voice of Mukamba*. The American Libraries Association selected it as one of the top books in 1998. The proverbs with which Mother graced my life appear in my book, *The School with No Walls: Where Lifelong Lessons Begin*, published in 1997.

Life is a journey with many hurdles to overcome. It isn't what you have or don't have that can help remove the hurdles in your life. Hard work, vision, determination, love for God and service to others remove all those hurdles, one at a time. You *can* live with less if you have something to live for.

A home can exist without buildings. One definition for the word "home" is, "The social unit formed by a family living together."[1] In the culture of the Kamba people of Kenya, where I was raised, "home" is sometimes synonymous with family. In Joshua 24:15 we read, ". . . as for me and my house, we will serve the LORD" (KJV). In this instance, the word "house" refers to Joshua's family.

From my godly mother, I learned to live by Joshua's words. Now I live in a modern house with modern conveniences in a typical suburban American neighborhood. My family enjoys material possessions, but these are not what give us a rich quality of life. What enriches us is our love for one another and our great faith and trust in God.

Endnote

1. "Home," *Merriam-Webster's Collegiate Dictionary*. Tenth edition (Springfield, MA: Merriam-Webster, Incorporated, 1996), p. 554.

Dr. Vincent Muli Wa Kituku, speaker, author, columnist and adjunct professor at Boise State University, has dedicated his life to nurturing the human spirit. A native of Kenya, he earned his Ph.D. from the University of Wyoming in 1991. Dr. Kituku is an award-winning storyteller and platform speaker who motivates audiences to identify and effectively deal with what he calls their "spiritual and social buffaloes."

Contact: Vincent Kituku
P.O. Box 7152,
Boise, ID 83707

Website: www.kituku.com
E-mail: Vincent@kituku.com

Attitudes, Words and Chocolate Chips

Karen R. Morerod

hocolate chips on the kitchen floor usually aren't a reason for celebration, but this day they were.

Our family was your typical suburban family. We had five children, and it seemed someone was always going somewhere, needing something or spilling something. Or two someones were needing a referee. Yes, we lived in the fast lane.

There's nothing inherently bad about that, unless things get out of control. I came to realize our home was at that point when I began listening more closely to the sounds in our home. What I heard was disturbing: impatient words and attitudes tossed about; or, at other times, just a rude and disrespectful tone of voice.

What really hit me, though, was that each time I heard offending comments from others, the words and attitudes seemed all too familiar. It appeared *I* was the driving force behind these attitudes. I saw how my selfishness had caused me to be short, curt and rude at times when things went awry. My impatience had been mounting month by month as I focused on the negative behavior of others. Consequently, other family members were also showing disrespect to others.

At my point of realization, three of the children were teenagers and the other two were younger but still able to display these inappropriate behaviors. I felt I had lost the race. I felt we had reached the point of no return. I wondered if it was possible to change our course now, or if I should go ahead and wave the white flag.

As my concern mounted, I took it to the Lord in prayer. It seemed the first person God chose to change was *me*! In response to my earnest prayer, God showed me that, as the concerned mother of this team, I needed to start modeling appropriate behavior if I expected anyone else to do the same.

As I continued in prayer about this, I sensed God granting me little victories. First, even though I still spouted impatient phrases, I would feel convicted immediately and ask for forgiveness. This heightened my awareness of the problem. My next victories came when, as I would start to speak unkindly, I was able to put the brakes on my attitude in the middle of an out-of-control lecture. After a period of time and continued prayer, I noticed more and more of my attitudes were changing, thus allowing for patience to take the lead.

I didn't know just how far along in this race I was until *that* day. I was making cookies, and unbeknownst to me, my six-year-old grabbed the bag of chocolate chips. The next noise was the pitter patter of chips spilling all over the kitchen floor. I turned, called his name sharply and started in with a once-familiar out-of-control lecture. As he looked up at me in surprise, I realized how long it had been since I had reacted so impatiently. In fact, my behavior seemed foreign.

I calmed down, but in spite of my temporary loss of control I still wanted to shout, *"Hallelujah!"* I realized impatience was indeed taking a back seat in my life. God was at work making impatience the exception instead of the rule.

No, our household still isn't perfect. But as we continue to race along in the fast lane, I see God continuing to work as I let Him lead. And I'm looking forward to the day when, even in the fast lane, our words and actions are as calm as a Sunday drive.

Karen Morerod, who resides in Kansas City, Kansas, is a homemaker and freelance writer. She learns daily lessons from her life as a pastor's wife and mother of five children. Karen teaches Sunday school and women's Bible studies where she is able to encourage others out of her own experiences.

E-mail: krm60@juno.com

When God Used Termites

Marie Asner

In the small northern town where I grew up, gambling and alcoholism were frequent scourges to many families. One industry—a sawmill—was the main employer in the town. As long as workers did their jobs, their employer didn't care what their family life was like.

Bob, one of the dashing young men in the area, wooed and married my mother's quiet cousin Anne. Soon their first child was born: a *girl*. This did not sit well with Bob. Over the next ten years, Anne had six children. The first three were daughters and then came sons, but by that time it was too late.

Money was needed for the growing family, and wages from the sawmill didn't fill the bill. Bob began to gamble and drink heavily. He worked eight-hour shifts at the mill, then drank with his buddies for hours before coming home. He would enter the house in a rage, flailing at everyone in sight, before eating dinner and falling asleep, only to start the cycle again the next day.

The family was not allowed to eat before he came home, so they went hungry for hours before eating dinner.

There was barely enough money for groceries, and of course Bob's "needs" came first—so my mother and her friends came to the rescue with secret food baskets left at the back of the property. The children would pretend to go out to feed the dog, and then sneak back into the house with pockets full of potatoes or eggs.

Once the neighbors complained to the only police officer in town of screams coming from the house. Not long after the officer's visit to deal with Bob, Anne had bruises on her face and arms and one child had a cut lip. No one ever called the police again for fear of Bob's reprisal against the family.

Our home became a place of refuge for Anne and her children when Bob was on one of his drunken rampages. His drinking and his gambling debts now virtually wiped out his paycheck.

When I was ten years old, a retired minister moved to our small town and bought an abandoned church and adjacent parsonage. He had a pension for his living expenses and decided to start a Protestant congregation there. The church was close to Anne and Bob's home.

One Sunday afternoon, when I was playing with the girls (my cousins) in their front yard, the minister came to call. He invited Anne and Bob to attend services and bring the children to Sunday school.

Bob angrily declared: "It would take me falling through the floor to bring me to church!"

One month later, when Bob got up in the middle of the night, it happened. As he stepped onto the floor, it gave way beneath him and he found himself hanging between the bedroom and the basement. The waist-

band of his underwear was snagged on the floor-
boards. Anne went to the neighbors' house for aid.
They took their time calling the policeman, who eventually arrived to find Bob still struggling to keep from
falling into the basement.

Hearing the commotion down the street, the minister came too.

"Well, Bob," he said, "Are you ready to come to
church now?"

With the policeman as a witness, Bob relented and
agreed to "try it." He was pried loose and taken to
the local doctor for treatment of cuts, bruises and
embedded splinters.

Word got around. Sure enough, the next Sunday,
Bob, Anne and the children were in church. Most of
the town turned out. They heard the pastor speak of
the power of God to heal lives (even working
through the termites that had caused the floor-
boards to break). Amazingly, this message pene-
trated Bob's mind, and he and Anne became regular
churchgoers. Bob eventually became Head Usher.

No more alcohol, beatings or gambling: the family
house became a real home! Bob lived twenty more
years and was a firm but gentle father and a good
provider. All six children completed high school
and/or college. Anne outlived Bob by ten years,
keeping herself active with organizations concerned
with women's rights and spousal abuse.

Whenever I think of God's power, I think of
Anne's survival through the ordeal of her marriage.
Having her husband transformed from a violent
drunk and gambling wastrel to a father who actually

provided for his children was a miracle. God, indeed, works in mysterious ways, even using the lowly termite.

Marie Asner is a church musician, poet, entertainment reviewer and freelance writer in the Kansas City area. She won the 1998 Grand Prize in Writing at the Kansas City Christian Writers Network Conference. Marie's poems were selected to launch Kansas City's 150th birthday celebration in 2000.

Contact: Marie Asner,
P.O. Box 4343,
Overland Park, KS 66204-0343

What Matters the Price of Gold?

Lola Gillebaard

I hate to polish silver. I also hate to see it tarnished. When the second hate overpowers the first, I groan, pull out the jar of silver polish, turn on the radio and then I rub.

That's what I was doing recently when the radio announcer blurted out the latest price of gold, followed by the price of silver.

My rubbing motion slowed. I gazed more fondly at the silver. No matter how much the price may fluctuate, I knew I was cleaning up a small fortune.

I rinsed the heavy coffee server with hot water and dried it carefully. Then I picked up my favorite piece: a silver utensil for brewing hot tea. On the end of the long handle rests an ornate windmill that turns when pushed. Hank's parents gave it to us many years ago. I watched the tiny windmill go round and round and thought fondly of those two unforgettable folks.

They were married in Amsterdam, Holland in 1920. Mama's wedding present to Papa was a real legacy, a watch sprinkled with diamonds and rubies that was made in 1790. It was a technological wonder for its time. When it was pressed, the watch would chime the time. The chime was as hearty as a tulip and always accurate. This precious heirloom had belonged to Mama's grandfather.

Papa's wedding gift to Mama was a lovely gold bracelet with diamonds clustered all the way around, even covering the safety catch. Like most married couples, Mama and Papa had their ups and downs, but they had a strong faith in God and deeply loved each other. They produced and raised five children. When the oldest child was fourteen years old, Holland became an occupied country for five years during World War II.

The German Occupation began in 1940. Soon after that, rationing of food began. The Gillebaard family, like most families in Amsterdam, learned to live with scarcity. The Dutch people began to buy anything of value, particularly gold, diamonds and silver, hoping these things would later buy them food.

In September of 1944, the Allied air invasion of Arnhem cut off the Dutch industrial west, which was the most densely populated portion of Holland. The resulting food rations for the Gillebaard family of seven were two pounds of sugar beets, two pounds of potatoes and one loaf of bread—each per week per person. Dutch guilders bought the rationed food and paid the rent. For any other purchase, inflation made money almost worthless.

My husband, Hank, was seventeen years old then. He weighed eighty-five pounds. His mama's sugar beet potato soup was mostly water by the middle of each week.

One night, after sending the children to bed hungry, Mama prayed a long time and then slipped something into Papa's pocket.

Papa protested. Mama insisted.

The next morning, Papa swapped Mama's beautiful gold and diamond bracelet on the black market for a goat—supposedly a milk goat. The goat was delivered in the middle of the night and put into the attic of the Gillebaard home.

Now Papa was a businessman, not a farmer. But that night he went to the attic with a footstool and a pail. He looked like a man who knew exactly what he was about. The truth was, Papa had never milked a cow, let alone a goat.

The goat was white, with electric blue eyes. Papa's eyes were electric blue too. The man and the animal glared at each other. Papa sat on the stool and pulled at what he hoped were the proper appendages for milk. The goat bleated loudly and took off for the farthest corner of the attic.

Papa picked up the pail and stool, walked over and placed the pail underneath the goat and pulled. The goat bleated again and kicked Papa in the stomach. Then the animal knocked over the pail and raced to the opposite corner of the room.

The family was waiting at the bottom of the steps as Papa came down. Beads of perspiration rolled off his neck. He turned up the empty pail and said,

"Look, there's not a drop of milk in here. That crazy goat is dry."

And then Papa started back up the steps. This time he was carrying an axe. He slammed the attic door behind him. They all heard him say, "I'm sorry I have to do this, goat."

Mama and the children listened to the clattering of the goat's hooves as it galloped back and forth across the floor, bleating frantically. In between bleats, we could hear Papa's determined footsteps and the sound of his voice as he talked to the goat. Then more bleats, more hooves, louder talking.

Finally, the goat's bleating drowned out the other sounds. The attic door opened. Papa backed through the door—still talking to the goat. He held the axe behind his back. His shirt was torn and his hand was bleeding.

"That idiot goat is alive and well," he said as Mama bandaged the hand in a piece of cloth.

Papa went next door. The neighbor had owned a butcher shop before meat had been withdrawn to the black market. The neighbor butcher killed and skinned the goat. His price was half the carcass. He did not split the carcass lengthwise. He took the bottom half.

And so Mama's priceless gold and diamond bracelet bought the Gillebaard family the top half of a milkless goat. Mama prepared delicious goat stew, goat hash and goat soup. The family gave thanks, feasted and rejoiced.

By February of 1945 the goat was remembered as a bounteous smorgasbord. The food rations had dwindled to half a loaf of bread and two potatoes per person per week.

Mama supplemented her family's meager diet with boiled tulip bulbs whenever she was lucky enough to find them. The weather was freezing. There was no wood or coal to burn, and the Gillebaards, like most Dutch people, were slowly starving.

One Sunday afternoon, Papa and one of his employees bicycled to the farmland outside the city of Amsterdam. They pedaled on bicycle rims—all rubber had been confiscated many months before.

They knocked on the door of every farmhouse. They asked each farmer if he had any food to sell. Papa revealed his precious antique gold watch, which he needed to trade for nourishment.

Each farmer examined the watch, listened to the chimes, shook his head, gave the watch back and said, "I've got gold coming out of my ears."

Papa and his employee turned up their coat collars against the wind and continued to cycle. At last they found a farmer who, though he wouldn't look at the watch, did look at the two men. Then he said, "What can you do?"

Papa's employee said, "I'm a carpenter." The farmer smiled and said, "There's work for you." The farmer was also without any fuel for heat. He ordered the employee to fill in every crack in the house to insulate against the cold. Papa helped as best he could.

Upon completion of the work, the farmer gave the two men four sacks of beans. As the two loaded the beans onto the bicycles, the light of the wintry day was fast disappearing.

The farmer said, "Let me see that watch." Papa's heart pounded. He proudly displayed the watch in the palm of his hand. He pressed for the chime. The farmer listened. He propped his hands upon his hips.

"I've got enough gold and diamonds to open a jewelry store of my own," he said, "but I'll give you a sack of beans for the watch."

Papa said, "Make it two."

The farmer said, "One sack of beans. That's it."

Papa thought about the seven stomachs he yearned to fill. Praying to God that someday he would be able to buy the watch back, he said sadly, "I'll take the beans."

The Gillebaard family survived and Papa eventually got his watch back. Papa told the story many times. He always ended by saying, "The love of family and the precious skills of labor are worth more than precious gold and silver."

And so it is today as then: What matters the price of gold and silver? In time of war or famine, what will they buy? A sack of beans? A milkless goat?

I turned off the radio and put the gleaming silver back where it belonged.

Choose my instruction instead of silver,
knowledge rather than choice gold.
(Proverbs 8:10)

Lola Gillebaard is a humorist who believes laughter is the handshake of good communication and that humor in business is serious business. She is an author, speaker and a past president of the Greater Los Angeles Chapter of the National Speakers Association. Lola conducts training seminars on humor in the workplace and is a frequent keynote speaker for corporate and convention audiences. She and her husband, businessman-sculptor "Hank" Gillebaard, live in Laguna Beach, California.

Website: www.laughandlearn.org
E-mail: lola@laughandlearn.org

Cross-Eyed and Tongue-Tied

Richard H. Harvey

I shall not die, but live,
and declare the works of the LORD.
(Psalm 118:17, KJV)

In a tumbledown shack that was called a parsonage in Grove City, Pennsylvania, a cross-eyed, tongue-tied "blue" baby boy was born to Emma and Henry Harvey. They were told that it was only a matter of hours before the baby would die.

Not convinced, the father went immediately to God in prayer and said, "Even though the physicians said it was impossible for us to have another child, You have given us one. Would You reveal to us what You have to say concerning our son?" Then, for an answer, he went, as usual, to God's Word.

In Psalm 118:17, God gave him this promise: "I shall not die, but live, and declare the works of the LORD." As far as that young father was concerned, it was a definite promise to him that the child would live

27

and serve the Lord. And my father was right—because over seventy years later, here I am! But in my early years, my father had to lean heavily on that promise. It was a tremendous struggle just for me to live.

When I was eleven months old, I contracted double pneumonia and whooping cough. A nurse who was visiting in the home and assisting my mother came and told my father that I had died. Father said, "Don't tell his mother. He's not dead." He knelt by my crib and reminded God of His promise until he was satisfied that God had answered prayer and the crisis was past.

When I was about a year old, my parents were sure that I was cross-eyed. It was not just a weakness, but something that looked permanent. So one day they clasped their hands over my crib and laid their hands on me and asked God to straighten my eyes. And He did it! (I'm homely enough now, but I'm sure I must have been far worse as a cross-eyed baby!)

Before I was three years old I had contracted black diphtheria, and again someone came and told my father that I had died. Father said, "Well, don't say anything to anybody." He went into the room, shut the door, knelt down by my bed, took hold of my hand, and there he stayed until I moved. He got up, thanked God and went and told my mother that I was all right.

Before I was four years old, a nurse visited our home. My parents said to her, "Our son seems to have normal intelligence." (Now, you may doubt that and think it parental prejudice, but that's what they said.) "But Richard won't talk. We can't get him to say anything."

I hadn't even said, "Mama" or "Daddy." Instead I had sounds for everything I wanted.

The nurse looked into my mouth and said, "Reverend Harvey, your son is very badly tongue-tied. There is a string at the roof of his mouth, as well as under his tongue."

When she left, my mother and father knelt beside me, laid their hands on me and prayed. Again my father quoted the promise, "I shall not die, but live, and declare the works of the LORD." He prayed, "Lord, You said not only that my son would live and not die, but that he would declare the works of the Lord. He cannot declare Your works with his tongue tied."

God loosed my tongue. Sometimes I think He did too good a job—for it has many times gotten me into trouble! I began to speak at four years and some of my relatives said I made up for it in the next two years. One of my uncles called me a windjammer!

At the age of six I was sent to school. I was there one week when I came down with measles and was sent home. At the end of the quarantine period I went back to school. I was in school three more days before I contracted the chicken pox. So I was kept home again for a stretch and after the quarantine period for that, I went back to school. Then it was scarlatina. Again I was kept home. My parents decided to wait until after the Christmas vacation to send me back. I returned but contracted typhoid fever. At the end of that stretch my parents decided I was too weak to go back to school. So in reality I didn't start school until I was seven!

About a year later I began to be conscious of the fact that I was a sinner. I was on my way out of school one day. It had snowed heavily that morning and the boys had made a slide in front of the school. I tried it, but my feet went out from under me. My head hit the sidewalk and out from my lips came an oath. I couldn't help but say to myself, "Isn't that strange! My father and mother don't swear. That must have come from the inside."

When my father asked me to say grace at the table, I knew God didn't hear me. When I prayed at family worship, I knew God didn't hear me. When I prayed at night before I went to bed, God was silent because there was sin in my heart and it was unconfessed. From the moment that oath slipped out, I was afraid I'd have an accident and die.

One day at a summer camp, sitting in the back of the tent, really not too interested in the meeting, I again became conscious of the guilt on my heart. When the preacher's invitation was given, I waited until the very last line of the last verse of the hymn. Then I walked down the sawdust aisle. I knelt at the altar, confessed my sins and gave my heart and life to Jesus Christ.

Only a person who has experienced this understands the great peace that comes. One seems lighter. Even nature takes on a new look. To some it seems that a heavy burden rolls away. Sin is gone and many fears disappear.

Soon after I took that step, our missionary conference began. With my newfound joy I had a great desire that all the boys and girls around the world would come to know Jesus Christ also. At the dinner table I asked my father if I could make a missionary pledge (a promise to give a specific amount of money within a specific period of time). His reply was characteristic: "Well, son, you can make a pledge if you pay it yourself, but don't expect me to help."

So I began to figure how much money I'd receive in a year's time from running errands and from gifts for special days. My total came to $8.50. After weighing the sacrifice of certain pleasures, I pledged $8.00, reserving 50 cents for refreshments at summer camp.

Soon after the missionary conference came Easter. At Easter, it was my parents' custom to give me 50 cents to purchase Easter candies for my basket. But I had figured that 50 cents into the amount I would receive. Therefore, I knew I had to put it into the missionary bank. It was not easy to do and though I did it, it was not done joyfully.

My father thought he might buy me one candy Easter egg, but decided against it, believing the sacrifice and discipline would do me good. I told my father some years later I was glad God was more merciful than *he* was, because God laid "my need" on the hearts of two French girls who worked for a wealthy family. Those girls competed to see which one could give me the most Easter gifts! They both brought me a cardboard box full of Easter goodies—the kind of boxes used to bring groceries home from the supermarket. If I took all the other Easter gifts received in my entire life, they would not compare with what those two girls gave me that night before Easter!

But that was not all. That same year God led a drugstore man to give me a bag of candy and chewing gum almost every day on my way home from school. Once in a while he would call me in to the soda fountain and tell me I could choose anything I wanted. Since a banana split was the finest and most expensive item on the glass behind his counter, a banana split was my request.

Thus, early in life I learned that one cannot outgive God. "Give, and it shall be given unto you; good measure, pressed down, and shaken together, and running over . . ." (Luke 6:38, KJV). That, I have found, is God's response to any sacrifice we ever make.

The pledge, of course, was paid on time!

From *70 Years of Miracles* by Richard H. Harvey,
© 1977, 1992 by Horizon Books.

Dr. Richard Harvey had a long and varied career as one of the founders of Youth for Christ International, as president of LeTourneau College, and as a pastor, district superintendent, church planter and evangelist. His life and ministry were accompanied by supernatural events, not the least of which were numerous decisions for Christ in response to his powerful preaching.

Believing for the Impossible

Doreen Hanna

Several years ago our family encountered a financial crisis that caused us to sell our home. My husband Chad and I were sitting in our kitchen pondering what we should do and where we should go when the phone rang. It was my parents.

They informed us that their renters had just given them notice and they wondered if we would like the opportunity to move into the rental house, which was located on the same piece of property as their home and my father's cabinet shop. We accepted without hesitation. Losing our own home was disappointing, but we were excited about moving to this small town in Arizona that would provide a more rustic and peaceful way of life.

Shortly after our arrival my father requested Chad's help to carry on his custom cabinet business during the time he would be laid up after a serious back injury. When he recovered (almost a year later), he felt well enough to step back into the business.

Chad, having experienced the joy of running a small business, decided he would go into business for himself. My father would continue to do custom cabinets while Chad went into home building. It all sounded good for both parties.

Upon Chad's exit from my father's place of business, my father claimed that Chad had taken items that were not his. He told others but did not confront Chad directly. When Chad heard secondhand about the accusation, he told my father he was sure he hadn't taken anything that wasn't his. In an attempt to "keep the peace" Chad asked my father to come to his shop and look over all that he had. If there was anything that was my father's, Chad said, he was welcome to take it and there would be no argument. My father never came.

Normally, we met with my folks every week or so for dinner. As time went on tension built between Dad and Chad, and when we'd get together everyone could feel it. Dad is by nature a talker, but when Chad would arrive in the same room Dad became silent. The tension caused one or the other couple to give excuses as to why we couldn't get together in a particular week. Weeks turned into months.

One day my father called and asked if he and my mother could come over and talk with us that evening. From the tone of his voice, I dreaded the thought of us getting together; I recognized in his tone a warning that "this isn't going to be good." Out of respect, though, I agreed to have them come over. I hoped that maybe Dad and Chad would finally talk things out.

When my parents arrived that evening, the first thing my father said was, "Chad, for the last three weeks I have been contemplating killing you!"

I was shocked! I could hardly believe what I was hearing. I knew my father had been struggling over the issue with Chad, but I hadn't realized how bitter he had become.

Right away my thoughts turned to a conversation my mother and I had just a few days prior to that meeting. She told me their home had been broken into three weeks before. As my mother reviewed the stolen goods report filed with the police, she noticed that my father had listed a handgun. She never knew that my father even had a gun until she saw it on the report. It was, to say the least, a startling revelation.

Now, with my dad's words about wanting to kill my husband ringing in my ears, I silently thanked God for his protection over all of us. I was convinced that God used the robbery in my parents' home to seize that gun out of my father's hand.

My thoughts were interrupted. I heard Chad tell my father to leave our home, and then heard my father tell us we weren't allowed to come to his. As my parents left our home that night my heart went out to my mother. She was as shocked as I. As they drove out the driveway my heart ached and I wondered what would happen. Yet I was relieved, knowing God had protected my father and Chad.

The next morning my mother called to say my dad had forbidden her to see us. We agreed to begin praying for reconciliation between Chad and my father. At the time I thought it would be impossible, but my mother's example of praying faithfully in the face of trials challenged *me* to keep praying. Over the next eight months she and I met clandestinely on a street corner or at the market, just to see each other face-to-face and collect a hug.

One day Mom called to tell me that my father was beginning to express feelings that he should take steps to reconcile with Chad. I was elated, but she made me promise not to tell Chad. A few weeks later, over our quiet breakfast together, Chad announced: "We are family and this can't go on; maybe I should go and talk to your dad." I could hardly believe what I was hearing. God was truly at work!

Several more weeks passed. Then early one morning I answered a knock at the door. I opened it to find my dad standing in the doorway. He asked if Chad was in, and Chad stepped forward. Dad then asked Chad's permission to come in, and Chad consented.

Without hesitation Dad looked Chad straight in the eye and said, "Chad, I . . . I've been trying to get things right with God for some time, but every time I pray, all I hear is that I need to come and ask for your forgiveness. I can't get things right with God until I get things right with you. Will you please forgive me?"

Chad was quiet momentarily, then he said, "Dad, will you forgive *me*?" They fell into each other's arms and began to weep.

Today we enjoy the blessing of spending time and sharing friendship, laughter and wisdom in my parents' home, and they in ours. I am still in awe of what God did in our lives—something I had once thought would be impossible!

"I am the LORD, the God of all mankind. Is anything too hard for me?" (Jeremiah 32:27)

 Doreen Hanna is a freeland writer and professional speaker. A graduate of CLASS (Christian Leaders Authors and Speakers Seminars), she speaks for women's luncheons, seminars and retreats. She and her husband, Chad, live in Redondo Beach, California.

E-mail: DoreenHanna@aol.com

Homeless No More

Cheri Peters

I have been all over the the United States and overseas working with at-risk youth who need the assurance of God's forgiving love. The miracles I have seen in youth rallies, prisons, churches, homeless shelters, camp meetings and even brothels have encouraged me to keep our ministry (True Step Ministries) going strong. It is awesome to see young people make commitments to God and to themselves. Best of all, I have seen people of all ages who once were wounded and living in their shame now released and saved.

Sometimes I ask the Lord, "Who am I to be helping others, when not so many years ago I myself was the one in desperate need of help?"

God always answers that earnest question with the same clear, firm reply: "Cheri, it is *because* of your wounded past that I can use you. You are able to relate to those who are hopeless, grieving, feeling guilty or in deep emotional pain because you've suffered all those things yourself."

The story of how I got from where I was then to where I am now is a miracle in itself.

I never felt the love of family. Unwanted and rejected before I was even born, I sought approval and love in all the wrong places. After I turned thirteen, I spent ten years of my life on the streets. I used a fake ID and became a barroom dancer. Drugs and alcohol were my daily companions. My world was ugly and my life was a mess. Everything and everyone around me seemed hopeless.

One day in desperation I came to the end of my rope. I seriously thought about suicide. *How should I do it?* I dumped the contents of my bedside drawer on the carpet. *What am I searching for?*

I kicked through the mess. A white envelope stuck out from the pile with my name in Mom's handwriting scrawled on the front. I ripped it open. Mom wrote about her childhood. She had never told me anything about her childhood. I shivered. It seemed as if I were staring in a mirror, reading my own story. When she wrote about her sadness, my eyes misted. I wanted to hold her, tell her I was sorry for her pain.

The paper she had written for a psychology class assignment told how my young teenage parents were overjoyed when my older sister Dedra, their first child, was born. When Dedra was only two months old my mom found herself pregnant again. Deep depression engulfed her. Everything changed. My dad started to drink. My parents began to argue. Mom withdrew from him and everyone. She attempted to self-abort but, in spite of her efforts, I was born.

"I hated her," she wrote. My heart plunged. *I was the "her" she wrote about.* In depression and anger she had rejected me. There was nothing I could have done to get acceptance or love from my mother or from the rest of my family. I dropped the paper, stunned. At last the truth.

A voice seemed to speak to me: "This was never about you." I looked around. I was alone.

What? It was never about me? Dizziness swept over me. *Never about me?* A new feeling tugged me upward away from my muddy pain, leaving bubbles of light and hope. *Maybe I'm not really a bad person.*

"I love you," the voice said.

"What? Who are you? Where?" I cried out loud.

Silence: warm and peaceful. I was loved.

What does this mean? What do I do? I wondered. *I must get out of here. I need a quiet place where no one does drugs, a place to think and sleep. But where? Who can I call? I don't know anyone who doesn't do drugs.*

Then I remembered Jake, a young man I had recently met who drank orange juice instead of alcohol and didn't use drugs. He had given me his phone number and said, "If I can ever help you, give me a call."

Jake took me up to his sister's mountain home in Placerville, California.

"It's a perfect place for you to rest," Jake said. "One thing, though," he added, "My sister's a very conservative Christian."

"What does that mean?"

"Well, my whole family is pretty straight. Nobody smokes, drinks or anything like that. It'll be different for you, *that's* for sure," he chuckled.

Jake introduced me to his sister, Donna, her husband and a large assortment of relatives. Donna was a middle-aged woman with short, wavy brown hair, a dimpled chin and discerning eyes. She welcomed and hugged me before I could shrink away.

"What's the topic of the study tonight?" someone asked, pulling out a Bible.

Jake whispered to me, "They meet together every Friday night to study the Bible and spend time together."

I felt sick. *What am I doing here? I feel so out of place.*

Everyone was kind. They tried to make me feel at ease. The next day, Donna took me on a walk in the foothills. Later, back at the house, I gazed out the window as the stereo softly played a Christian music tape with Sandi Patti's lilting, soothing voice. Tears slid down my cheeks.

Donna came and sat beside me. We listened silently for a long time. Then she spoke softly about her experience with Jesus and His love. "God knows us. He knows our condition," she said. "More importantly, even the best of us is full of sin. No sin is worse than another."

"What?" I lashed out. "You have no clue what you're talking about. You can't expect me to believe that all sins are the same. That God looks at me in the same way He looks at . . . at . . . you."

Donna said nothing.

Over the next few days, Donna asked me gently about my childhood, my rejection and fears, my hurts and loneliness. She listened compassionately, shedding tears when I told her of the pain and ugliness of my life. She talked of God's forgiveness and told me how God's son, Jesus, died for us to bring us back to God. I listened politely, but thought under my breath: *If you really knew me, you'd kick me out of your home.*

I'd never spoken of the awful things that had been part of my life. Now I was pouring out the sickening details to someone I hardly knew. I looked at Donna, expecting the same disgust in her eyes that I felt for myself. Donna looked back, her face mirroring my pain, her warmth surrounding me. When I started to cry, her arms held me fast.

The physical pains of withdrawal were becoming manageable, but a deeper, emotional pain was awakening.

"Lord, help me," I whispered.

"What did you say?" Donna asked.

"Oh, I was just thinking out loud." I smiled. This was going to be tougher than I thought.

Terrifying memories of experiences I had long blocked out came flooding back into my consciousness. I told her everything, all the sordid details, fully expecting her to react in revulsion. But compassion, not judgment, glowed in her eyes. I realized I kept getting myself into messes when all I really wanted was to be safe and loved. Did she understand that?

A forgotten hurt lumped up in my throat when I related the suicide death of one of the barroom dancers at the club I worked in and how uncaring everyone at the club seemed to be about it. I pounded my fist into my hand. "When you were with each other, it was like family, everyone so close. One big happy family. But walk out the door, die or just disappear off the face of the earth, it was as if you never existed at all."

I whirled around and hid my face from Donna. "Donna, is that just the way life is?"

"No, that's not the way life is. You have seen a very small part of life, of human nature. A part of life no one should experience."

She came and stood beside me. "Cheri, will you pray with me?"

"There's nothing I want more."

"Dear Father, please show Cheri Your love. She has seen such ugly things in her life. Please show her the beauty of Your love, Your mercy. Give her hope and the courage to heal, to trust in You. Send Your Holy Spirit to give her the wisdom and ability to listen to You. Thank You for all the promises You have given us, especially the promises that You will give us a new heart and a new mind to replace the old one that has been so damaged. Thank You, Lord."

"Donna, what did you mean about promises for a new heart?"

"In the Bible in Ezekiel 36:26-27, God promises this: 'I will give you a new heart and put a new spirit in you; I will remove from you your heart of stone and give you a heart of flesh. And I will put my Spirit in you.' "

A spring of light welled up inside me. These were words of life; these words were my only hope. *Oh, God, give me this new heart, this new spirit.*

I felt a sweet trickle seeping through my soul and the warm flow of faith, hope and love filled me. My heart, freed from numbness, frothed with wonder. *God, You*

love me? Yes, You do love me! You have always loved me.
Love unconditional, undeserved and completely mine!

I stayed at Donna's home for more than a week. I wolfed down everything I could about God, Jesus and the Holy Spirit. I couldn't get enough. There was so much I had to learn—so many changes to make.

Where should I start? Education. God led me to get my GED (the equivalent of a high school diploma) and to go on to nursing school. This was such a radical change of lifestyle for me that only a miracle from God could have made it possible.

While attending school, I had a job at a state hospital where I worked with developmentally disabled children in the Down's Syndrome unit. I know the Lord placed me there because I needed to be loved, and those kids loved me to death. Their unconditional love was water to my thirsty soul. I went to school full-time, worked full-time and studied the Bible with a group of new Christians. I was constantly amazed at how God directed my new life.

I wish I could say my faith and trust in God always stayed strong and constant but unfortunately it didn't. There was a time when I fell away again, but God sent a friend from my Bible study group to encourage me and remind me of God's promises. She urged me to let Him revive my faith. I did, and He did.

Today my life is exciting and full. My loving, supportive husband, Brad, knows my past and loves me anyway. We have a beautiful daughter. As an art therapist in a hospital, working with high-risk kids through the school district, I am a well-respected member of the community. I have a national radio ministry and I travel the globe, speaking to the lost, lonely and downtrodden, giving them hope, sharing my testimony and my exuberant belief in God's forgiveness and His healing, saving love.

I am happier now than I have ever been. I have a family at home and a loving family in my church. But in spite of my joy, God has shown me that I am still homeless: this world is not my home. Someday Jesus will come for me. On that day, I will look into the eyes of God and hear Him say, "I love you, Cheri. Welcome home!"

Cheri Peters is founder of True Step Ministries, a ministry working with at-risk people. She is also a public speaker and hosts a television show "Teen Pathways" and a radio show "The Journey Home." She has authored two books, *Miracle from the Streets* and *More Miracles from the Streets.* She says her greatest gifts in her life are her husband Brad and her daughter Jaci. They have recently opened STAR Ranch (Saving Those At Risk), a ministry for youth near Boise, Idaho.

Website: www.truestep.org

Section 2

Brothers and Sisters

*Be kind and compassionate to one
another, forgiving each other, just as
in Christ God forgave you.
(Ephesians 4:32)*

Little Sister to the Rescue

David O. Carter

I was more curious than concerned that Friday afternoon when I came home from school and found my little sister sitting on the couch, holding the hand of an old woman and whispering words of comfort to her.

The little lady, not much bigger than my seven-year-old sister, looked cozy and content. A soft blanket covered her thin shoulders, and on her tiny feet she wore my sister's pink fuzzy slippers.

Before I could ask, Diane began excitedly to explain. "Davey, this is Mary. Mary Matthews. I found her walking barefoot and in her nightgown, and I talked to her, and she's lost and confused, and she has a son who never visits her and she's very lonely, and I thought 'What would Jesus do?' and I brought her home."

Her big brown eyes sought approval.

I wasn't particularly surprised. It seemed Diane was always bringing home strays. Mostly dogs. Little dogs, big dogs, once a ferocious-looking dog (but actually a gentle one as it turned out). "But he followed me," she would say—which was true, although sometimes they followed at the end of a string. "Can I keep him? He's lost."

And not just dogs—Diane also brought home kittens, rabbits, ducks, birds with broken wings. Little sister always found a place in our home for them. All that mattered was that they needed a friend.

Our mother, a writer who worked at a weekly newspaper, wasn't home that afternoon, so I had to take charge.

"You did just the right thing, honey," I assured her. "Now I want you to keep Mary comfortable for a little while longer. I think I know where she lives, and the people there will be very worried."

The Golden Years Rest Home was only a few blocks away, so when I arrived and saw the police car parked at the curb and a small crowd of curious neighbors milling about, I knew I was right. Mrs. Matthews did live there and had wandered away.

As I entered the lobby of the rest home to tell my news, the place was full of noise and confusion. Everyone talked at once. Most of the noise was coming from a red-faced man who was shouting at no one in particular: "I'm a busy man and I don't have time for this nonsense. Find my mother! I don't want to hear excuses—just find her!"

He saw me and shouted, "What do you want, boy? You don't belong here! Get out!"

Startled, I blurted out, "The missing lady—I know where she is!" I guess I was yelling, too, because suddenly the office grew quiet and everyone was looking at me.

"My little sister found her." My voice cracked with excitement and a touch of pride. "She's at my house."

The man who had been yelling now spoke quietly. "Where is she? Where's my mother? Take me to her. Please!"

"It's just a few blocks," I said, "but first you'd better get her some clothes. She's in her nightgown."

The man's dark look sent an attendant rushing from the lobby. He was back shortly with a hastily packed overnight suitcase.

"Let's go, son," Mr. Matthews said. "Get in the car."

Mr. Matthews remained silent for the short ride as I repeated everything my little sister had told me, even about Diane wondering what Jesus would do. Now his expression was one of appreciation, tempered by sadness.

When I opened the front door he rushed in ahead of me, crossed the room and knelt before the small figure on the couch. "Are you all right, Mother?" he said softly. He took her hand into his. "I'm here now."

Reassured by her sweet smile, he turned to my sister and gently said, "Thank you, little girl. Thank you!"

"I'm Diane," my sister replied, an obvious note of disapproval in her voice. "Your mother said she ran away 'cause she was always lonely and 'cause nobody ever comes to see her. I'm going to be her friend and I'll visit her lots of times." Her voice was defiant and her eyes brimmed with tears.

After a long pause, Mr. Matthews spoke. His voice was hoarse with emotion. "Diane, you taught me a lesson today. Something's wrong when business becomes more important than people. I realize I've been lonely too, and selfish. Starting today, things are going to be different."

Mrs. Matthews face beamed as her son helped her to her feet, gave her a gentle hug and said, "Let's go home, Mother. We're going to be a family again."

About two weeks later my little sister received in the mail a lovely framed parchment. On it were these words:

WHAT WOULD JESUS DO?

David O. Carter writes light verse and short, whimsical stories and "fillers." His work has appeared in national magazines and he has won several writing prizes and awards. A native of Michigan, he has lived most of his life in the Bay area of Northern California.

A Sister's Shadow

Christine Foster

My sister and I are opposites. We're not just different, we're at polar extremes in many ways. Joanne is an extrovert, I'm an introvert; Joanne is an optimist, I'm a pessimist (although I prefer the term "realist"). Joanne likes gardening and old musicals. I like rodeos and stock car racing.

Being the younger sibling by two years, I grew up in my big sister's shadow. We had a continuous competition going on between us, and Joanne seemed better than me in every way. I was average, Joanne was not. She was above average. She was an A+ student, she was popular and she was pretty. Although my parents were careful never to compare us, it was shaming and hurtful whenever a teacher would ask me why I couldn't be more like my older sister.

In our youth we both took piano lessons—alas, just one more area in which Joanne excelled over me. I remember the day when I sat at our old upright piano, struggling to master one of my practice pieces. Extremely frustrated and close to tears, I finally gave up and retreated to my bedroom. After a few moments I heard my sister at the piano. She was sight-reading the piece I had just been laboring over, and she was playing it perfectly! I was so discouraged that I quit taking piano lessons altogether. As for games, against Joanne I was a chronic and guaranteed loser. .

When we fought as children it was emotionally explosive, and as adults little changed except perhaps that forgiveness came slower and less often, if it came at all.

For many years we lived very separate lives until a series of events brought us back under the same roof. Joanne and I had both married unbelieving and ungodly men. When they both left us, each of us with a small child, we had no other recourse than to live together for a while. Sadly, at a time in our lives when we should have been encouraging and supportive of each other, we bickered and argued instead.

After one year Joanne moved away to a school where she could complete her teaching degree. Then she went on to work in a Christian school teaching grades three through six. In the meantime, I began to write.

When I finished my first novel I was excited about the accomplishment, for it had been a lifelong dream of mine to write a book. I knew Joanne was proud of me as well, but I didn't realize the extent until she and some fellow teachers stopped by one night on their way to a conference. Joanne had told them about the book I had written, and even before introductions were made they were asking me about the book. As I explained a little about it to them I could see my sister standing off to the side, beaming at me.

A short time later I ran into some mutual friends of ours and they inquired about Joanne's doings. I found myself giving them a glowingly complimentary report on her accomplishments. It was then I realized how very proud I was of Joanne.

The following day I went to see Joanne. I told her how much I admired her and what I had said about her to our friends. At first she eyed me suspiciously, but it took only a moment for her to see my sincerity. She was visibly touched by my words of encouragement. Her eyes were brighter and her smile was wider.

For years I blamed my sister for many of my shortcomings and failures. Instead of being appreciative of her gifts and talents, I felt as though they had been the cause of my lack of confidence and achievement. When Joanne played my difficult piano piece effortlessly, instead of allowing the incident to defeat me I should have used it to strengthen my resolve and determination to conquer the piece.

I realize now that we are both equal in the eyes of God and that He is the source of our true worth. I have also come to understand that my sister has her own weaknesses and insecurities, just as I have mine.

As for me . . . well, I realize that in spite of all our diversities, my sister and I aren't really so different after all.

Christine Foster has written and published a novel entitled *Refuge*. She has also created a Christian comic book series with her husband, Craig Foster, who is an artist. Christine and her husband and daughter reside in Havelock, Ontario, Canada.

E-mail: sncfoster@nexicom.net
Website: www.craigfoster.com/foster_art

The Very Treasure

Janey DeMeo

It was a deliciously scorching afternoon on the Italian Riviera. With mountains behind me and the vibrant turquoise sea before me, I marveled at how the bright sun infiltrated my imagination, evoking an almost magical mirage.

I squinted at the serene scene before me and watched my daughter Rachéle-Claire swimming in the surf. It seemed as if I were watching a mermaid. Her long, golden, sun-streaked hair caressed the curves of the crystal waves as she swam, daintily bobbing up and down in the gentle surf.

It was an ironic illusion. As peaceful as my daughter appeared in this picturesque scene, Rachéle-Claire's attitude that morning had been quite the opposite. No onlooker at the seaside could have imagined the struggle she had been experiencing as her ten-year-old mind was exploring preteen independence.

Gleefully bopping in the waves next to her was her vivacious five-year-old brother Francesco, his bronzed skin blending with the distant brown rocks. The crisp echo of splashing waves, mingled with the children's peals of laughter, made a happy melody.

As the children interacted so playfully, who would have thought that, only a few hours before, I had been wearily umpiring their fight for the umpteenth time that morning? Here in Postcardland the "I hate my sister!" fire-and-ice syndrome had melted and rolled away with the waves. My husband, Louis, sat silently reading beside me, and all seemed so perfect.

But this idyllic scene belied my melancholy. I wondered why every morning had to begin with a battle. That very morning had begun with the usual morning squabbles. Why did my children always have to fight in spite of prayer and time in God's Word together?

Child rearing seems so difficult at times. And why did all those endless "how to" methods on Christian child training leave me so frustrated? I glanced again at my children playing peacefully in the surf, and sighed, "Heaven help me raise these children!" It was the sincere cry of a worn-out mother's heart.

Suddenly, my pondering was interrupted by some pretty stones that my five-year-old plopped on the sand in front of me.

"Look, Mama! I found some *very* treasure!" Francesco proclaimed excitedly.

"Lovely, son!"

'That's so cute!" my husband whispered in my ear. "He thinks *buried* treasure is *very* treasure!"

"I know," I responded. "I was teaching the children the parable of the buried treasure in Matthew

13, and ever since then he's called it *very* treasure. I never corrected him because I think it's so cute!"

"And here's some more, Mama!" our son interjected. Arranging the different colored stones into three piles on my towel, he pointed to each one and explained:

"Now here's the treasure; these ones are the *very* treasure, and those are the *very, very* treasure!"

My jaw was bulging trying to retain my laughter. We did not dare offend this serious little treasure hunter by laughing. But with concealed amusement, my whole spirit felt lighter. Life somehow seemed simpler, and the preciousness of my own little treasures more apparent.

I thought of the Scripture verse that says, "It is the glory of God to conceal a matter; to search out a matter is the glory of kings" (Proverbs 25:2).

I then realized that we parents are like kings reigning over our household. Little kings, under the Great King! We glorify Him as parents as we do our part in seeking to discover the very treasure of godly child rearing. It may be buried under layers of exhaustion, weaknesses, inadequacies and genetic incapacities. It has been concealed since before time began, but is revealed to all who seek (see Matthew 7:7). God's Word is an eternal source of wisdom waiting to be unveiled by the seeking heart—and to be experienced by those willing to pay the price!

That day on the beach with my children, I remembered a verse I'd read in Jeremiah 15:19 about separating "the precious from the vile" (KJV). God wants us to find precious things in every day, *very* treasures, even amidst the vile. He wants us to discover the lighter side of walking in a sometimes heavy world by seeking treasures in every circumstance. That day on the beach, I found treasure in the cute expressions of my own little child.

The kingdom of heaven is like treasure hidden in a field. (Matthew 13:44)

Janey DeMeo is the wife of Pastor Louis DeMeo, founder of their local church, a Christian day school and L'Institut Theologique, a Bible college in Uchaud, France. They have worked as missionaries in Europe, Africa, India and North America. Janey is president of Sauvez les Enfants in France and Orphans First in the United States; both are foundations devoted to helping suffering children. Janey, who is British, authored *Mon Dieu, Cez Enfants*, a parenting book published in France, and her articles have appeared in American and French Christian magazines.

Website: www.ggwo.org/orphansfirst
E-mail: LDeMeo@compuserve.com

A Brother's Lesson

Christopher de Vinck

I grew up in the house where my brother was on his back in bed for almost thirty-three years, in the same corner of his room, under the same window, beside the same yellow walls. Oliver was blind, mute. His legs were twisted. He didn't have the strength to lift his head nor the intelligence to learn anything.

Today I am an English teacher, and each time I introduce my class to the play about Helen Keller, "The Miracle Worker," I tell my students about Oliver. One day, during my first year of teaching, a boy in the last row raised his hand and said, "Oh, Mr. de Vinck. You mean he was a vegetable."

I stammered for a few seconds. My family and I fed Oliver. We changed his diapers, hung his clothes and bed linen on the basement line in winter, and spread them out white and clean on the lawn in the summer. I always liked to watch the grasshoppers jump on the pillowcases.

We bathed Oliver. Tickled his chest to make him laugh. Sometimes we left the radio on in his room.

We pulled the shade down over his bed in the morning to keep the sun from burning his tender skin. We listened to him laugh as we watched television downstairs. We listened to him rock his arms up and down to make the bed squeak. We listened to him cough in the middle of the night.

"Well, I guess you could call him a vegetable. I called him Oliver, my brother. You would have liked him."

One October day, when my mother was pregnant with Oliver, her second son, she was overcome by fumes from a leaking coal-burning stove. My oldest brother was sleeping in his crib, which was quite high off the ground so the gas didn't affect him. My father pulled them outside, where my mother revived quickly.

On April 20, Oliver was born. A healthy looking, plump, beautiful boy.

One afternoon, a few months later, my mother brought Oliver to a window. She held him there in the sun, the bright good sun, and Oliver looked directly into the sunlight, which was the first moment my mother realized that Oliver was blind. My parents, the true heroes of this story, learned with the passing months that blindness was only part of the problem. So they brought Oliver to Mt. Sinai Hospital in New York for tests to determine the extent of his condition.

The doctor said that he wanted to make it very clear to both my mother and father that there was absolutely nothing that could be done for Oliver. He didn't want my parents to grasp at false hope. "You could place him in an institution," he said.

"But," my parents replied, "he is our son. We will take Oliver home, of course."

The good doctor answered, "Then take him home and love him."

Oliver grew to the size of a ten-year-old. He had a big chest, a large head. His hands and feet were those of a five-year-old, small and soft. We'd wrap a box of baby cereal for him at Christmas and place it under the tree; pat his head with a damp cloth in the middle of a July heat wave.

Oliver was the weakest, most helpless human being I ever met, yet he was one of the most powerful human beings I have ever met. He could do absolutely nothing except breathe, sleep and eat, yet he was responsible for action, love, courage and insight. When I was small my mother would say, "Isn't it wonderful that you can see?" And once she said, "When you go to heaven, Oliver will run to you, embrace you, and the first thing he will say is 'Thank you.' " I remember too my mother explaining to me that we were blessed with Oliver in ways that had not been clear to her at first.

So often parents are faced with a child who is severely retarded, but who is also hyperactive, demanding or wild, who needs constant care. Many people have little choice but to place their child in an institution. We were fortunate that Oliver never knew what his condition was. We were blessed with his presence, for it was a true presence of peace.

When I was in my early twenties I met a girl and fell in love. After a few months I brought her home to meet my family. When my mother went to the kitchen to prepare dinner, I asked the girl, "Would you like to see Oliver?" for I had told her about my brother.

"No," she answered.

Soon after, I met Roe, a lovely girl. She asked me the names of my brothers and sisters. She loved children. I thought she was wonderful. I brought her home after a few months to meet my family. Soon it was time for me to feed Oliver. I remember sheepishly asking Roe if she'd like to see him. "Sure," she said.

I sat at Oliver's bedside as Roe watched over my shoulder. I gave him his first spoonful and his second. "Can I do that?" Roe asked with ease, freedom and compassion, so I gave her the bowl and she fed Oliver one spoonful at a time.

The power of the powerless. Which girl would you marry? Today Roe and I have three children.

Christopher de Vinck is the author of *The Power of the Powerless, Only the Heart Knows How to Find Them*, and the devotional *Simple Wonders*. He has been contributing devotionals to Guideposts for six years, and his writings and his columns have appeared in the *Wall Street Journal*, *Reader's Digest* and the *New York Times*. He lives with his family in Pompton Plains, New Jersey.

Half Mine, Half Yours

Brenda Blanchard

"Daddy, I want that row," I demanded, pointing at a choice section of the garden. "Can I have it?"

"Well . . ." he began.

"That's not fair," Shelly interrupted with a scowl on her tanned face. She turned to Mom. "Mom, she always gets first choice."

"Now, girls, let's not argue," Dad said. "There's plenty of garden for everyone." He grabbed the shovel and looked over at Mom with a smile that seemed to hold some secret between them.

Mom sorted through the seed packets while Dad tilled the soil. Shelly and I stood watching them in sullen silence. Although I was the older sister, Shelly was taller. We glared at each other, each knowing a sure victory for either of us was hardly likely.

After a few more impassioned appeals to Mom and Dad, which they ignored, I walked to the row of freshly plowed ground and drew a line with my finger right down the middle of the row.

"That's my half," I said indicating the right side and then the left, "and that side there is yours." We were used to halving just about everything, including our room.

"Fine, but don't you cross the line with any of your seeds," Shelly retorted. She bent down, picked up a stick and drove it vehemently into the ground on top of my fingerprint.

We grumpily halved the next two rows as well, giving each of us a fairly sizable piece of land. We stood back and surveyed our halves. No serious arguments arose, an indication that the halves were just about equal.

However, nothing else between us ever seemed quite equal. Her beauty surpassed mine, but my popularity and ability to make good grades exceeded hers. Somewhere along the way, we had forgotten the joy of being those cheerful little sisters who played dolls together and attended make-believe tea parties.

"Come on, girls," Dad said, "Let's get started. Head on over to your mom and get your seeds."

Shelly rushed over to the packets Mom had set out on the table. I pulled a folded paper from my hip pocket and opened it carefully. It contained a diagram of how I wanted my garden to be laid out. Of course, now I needed to change it since my row had been cut in half.

I wanted my garden to have a beautifully manicured appearance. I had planned a visually appealing descending stair effect. This would be accomplished by placing corn on one end of the row and radishes, the shortest vegetable at full growth, on the opposite end. The vegetables in between would be placed according to height as listed on the seed packets. Sitting at the table, I quickly scratched off several plants in each seed group so my stair-step idea would still work.

Shelly grabbed some seeds and rushed back to her half of our tilled rows. "Dad, will you help me?" she squealed.

Dad gave her pointers on how deep to plant each seed and then he dug a hole. "Drop one in," he said. He dug another hole about six inches from the first hole and said, "Again."

Shelly dropped another seed.

I sat at the table, examining my seeds one by one. If I noticed anything questionable, like an odd shape or color, that seed immediately became "unacceptable" for my garden. Mom watched me for a while, then shook her head and scurried to help Dad before the daylight slipped away.

Finally, I had all my seeds selected and sorted to my satisfaction. Shelly returned to the table and collected more seeds, with no rhyme or reason to her selection.

"Don't you want to make sure they're good first?" I asked disdainfully.

"No."

Gathering my seeds, I walked to my plot of fertile land. Shelly was on her knees, her face covered with dirt smudges. Her darkened hands worked the soil as her taunting words filled the air.

"I've only got one more row to go. I'm almost finished and you're just getting started." She stood up, chuckled and casually wiped her hands on her clothes.

"Don't worry about me," I snapped. "I'll be finished before the sun goes down and my garden will be a lot nicer than yours."

Shelly put her hand over her eyes and peered at the sun rapidly sinking toward the horizon. As she moved to her final row, she started whistling the "Whistle While You Work" tune.

I knew she was trying to annoy me. It worked, but I ignored her and slowly put on my gardening gloves.

"Dad," I yelled, "I've got corn here. How deep should I plant it?"

"About four inches will be fine," he replied. "A hand length apart is good."

Meticulously, I measured each hole I dug, using a notch on a stick to get the correct depth. Then I used the width of my hand to get the exact distance between each plant. I was only part way through my first row when I felt a tap on my shoulder.

"I'm finished," Shelly exclaimed, beaming. "You want some help?"

"Thanks, but no thanks," I shot back. The cheerful glow in her face faded. "Oh, OK, OK, but . . ." I growled as she bent down to dig a hole.

I was going to tell her the guidelines for my garden, but God must have put His hand over my mouth, because for some unknown reason I kept still. Shelly measured one hand from my last hole.

I smiled with smug delight. She really was going to do it my way.

She crawled in front of me digging the holes with her bare hands to the stick notch depth. I followed her with my perfect little seeds, placing one seed carefully into each hole and covering it gently with the soil Shelly had dug up. On the last row, I traded places with her.

Looking to the sky, I guessed we had another twenty minutes. I looked at Shelly; she understood the pressure I had created for myself, and didn't utter a word. Suddenly I realized that eyeballing the planting would be much faster and not nearly as much work. With a loud chuckle, I hurled the measuring stick as far as I could throw it.

With a playful grin, Shelly grabbed my hands and pulled off my gloves. "A little dirt never hurt anyone," she said softly. "Just feel God's good, sweet earth. It has a secret."

A secret? I thought skeptically. I looked at my clean hands and then at Shelly's dirt-smudged hands, face and clothes. She looked like she belonged to the soil.

"Come on. Just try it." Her eyes pleaded for me to stop being stubborn.

I pursed my lips and dropped reluctantly to my knees. Scooping up a mound of dirt, I let the fine particles slowly sift through my fingers. It felt soft and slightly damp.

"Funny, but dirt smells clean." I commented. Shelly nodded and smiled.

I shoveled up another pile and threw it into the air, watching it fall gracefully on my already planted rows. The extra dirt didn't seem to alter the design.

I dug the remaining holes with my bare hands. The dirt conformed to the sides of the hole as I kneaded my fingers deeper. The ground came to life beneath my fingers and I felt the inviting warmth, almost as if it had a soul.

Much as I didn't want to admit it, Shelly was right. God's earth does hold a secret—a secret that can only be learned when one's pulse flows into it, when it is touched and held in our bare hands. There's a message of love hidden deep within the soil; just as God's forgiving love lies deep within each of our hearts and must be personally touched to be understood.

As days went by and turned into weeks, our half rows started sprouting leaves and stalks of vegetables, but not in unison. Some leaves peeked their heads out a week earlier than their neighboring plant. When the late bloomers emerged, they caught up to the others and occasionally even grew taller.

All the while, Shelly and I watered the plants and pulled weeds together. We crossed each other's halves without giving the offense any special notice. Love and laughter bubbled up from our hearts, and now the long-awaited smiles of remembrance graced our faces.

Finally, it was time to harvest. Standing side by side, we looked at our garden with shared pleasure. We looked at each other with rekindled love, knowing the secret Mom and Dad had hoped we would find. Our beautiful garden and our sisterly relationship grew the way God wanted—with a little help from the earth's touch. At last we sisters were friends again.

Brenda Blanchard lives in Converse, Texas. She is a published freelance writer, part-time high school teacher, newsletter chairman for SANE (San Antonio Northeast Aglow International) and founder of Sisters in Christ Bible Study group. Her byline has appeared in *Women Alive*, *The Gem*, *God's Little Rule Book*, several newspapers and as a staff writer for *Bridges* romance magazine. Brenda is a member of Christian Writers Group, Austin Writers Guild and American Christian Writers.

E-mail: ZBGP1@aol.com

A Brother's Love

Diana L. James

She pulled back on the ropes, making the homemade swing fly higher and closer to the leafy branches of the tall sycamore tree. The breeze swished cool against her cheeks. She was five years old and, at that moment, stomping mad at her eleven-year-old brother, David.

How could he have been so mean? she asked herself, remembering how he had made a face and called her a "big baby" at the breakfast table. *He hates me*, she thought, *just because I took the last muffin out from under his nose. He hates me!*

The swing carried her up so high that she could see for miles. It was fun looking down at the farmyard below. Her red sweater flashed brightly in the morning sunlight. She stopped thinking about being mad at her brother and began to sing a swinging song.

On a distant hill behind the swing, a huge bull with long, sharp horns watched the red sweater flashing in the sunlight. The bull had broken out of his pasture.

He snorted and scraped the ground with his hoof. Then he lowered his massive head and began lumbering across the field toward the red sweater he saw swinging back and forth beneath the sycamore tree.

Meanwhile, David was in the barnyard feeding the chickens. He looked out and saw his little sister on the swing. *Sisters are a pain in the neck*, he thought to himself. Then suddenly he saw the bull charging across the field, heading straight for his sister. Without a second thought, David screamed as loud as he could, "Look out behind you. Get out of there! RUN!"

His sister didn't hear him; she just kept on singing and swinging. The bull was halfway across the field and closing in fast. David's heart pounded. It was now or never. He ran across the chicken yard, jumped the fence and dashed toward his sister. He ran faster than he had ever run before.

Grabbing one of the ropes, David jerked the swing to a stop, tumbling his sister sideways to the ground only a second before the snorting bull charged at the place where she had been. She let out a terrified yell. The bull spun around, scraping the ground again with his hoof. He lowered his head to charge again.

David yanked on one sleeve of the red sweater and then the other. Pulling it off his sister, he flung the sweater as far away as he could. The bull followed it. With horns and hooves, he ripped it into a hundred shreds of red yarn, while David half dragged, half carried his frightened sister to safety.

I was that little girl, and ever since that day, I just laugh when my brother calls me a "big baby." He can't fool me—I know he loves me. He doesn't have

to face a charging bull to prove it. But I'll never forget the day he did.[1]

* * *

The above story first appeared in *Chicken Soup for
the Kid's Soul*. Although I was only five years old at
the time of the incident described, I distinctly remember my mother's words to David and me on that
day. "I pray every day that God will protect you both
and that the two of you will always be good friends,"
our mother told us, as she kissed us good-bye and
left us there that summer day to spend another week
on her friend's farm while she was away at work.

The years have gone by and there have been other
times, less dramatic, when my brother has come to
my rescue or proved his love for me in a hundred different ways.

Now, to be honest, there have been times when he
was annoyed with me, or when he disagreed with me
(and vice versa). David and I have had times of separation because of geography or lifestyle. My Christian
beliefs are similar to my mother's, while David has followed quite a different path and has only lately begun
to take an interest in learning more about Jesus.

But the differences between us have never seemed
to matter as far as our brother-sister relationship is
concerned. Mother's prayer was beautifully answered:
my brother and I have always remained close, and I
know I can always depend on my brother's love.

"A Brother's Love" by Diana L. James, ©1998 by
Diana L. James. First appeared in *Chicken Soup*

for the Kid's Soul, published by Health Communications, Inc., Deerfield Beach, FL.

Diana L. James is the editor/compiler of *Bounce Back*, *Bounce Back Too*, *Teens Can Bounce Back* and this book, all four published by Horizon Books. Her stories and articles have also appeared in numerous magazines and fifteen book compilations. She speaks for churches, writers' conferences and Christian women's groups. Diana is founder and past President of Christian Writers of Idaho, and is radio host of "Encouraging Words," an inspirational radio interview program heard daily throughout southwestern Idaho and easter Oregon on KBXL-FM 94.1, Boise.

Website: www.dianajames.com
E-mail: dianajames@aol.com

Section 3

Marriage

. . . Whatever is true, whatever is noble, whatever is right, whatever is pure, whatever is lovely, whatever is admirable—if anything is excellent or praiseworthy—think about such things.
(Philippians 4:8)

A Missionary Romance

David C. Thompson, M.D.

I have a picture to prove that when I was fourteen months old I was present at the Mitchells' oldest daughter's first birthday. Of course, I don't remember anything about that encounter, but I do remember meeting Archie and Betty Mitchell in 1954 when I arrived at the Dalat School for Missionary Children in Dalat, Vietnam at the tender age of six.

Mrs. Mitchell was my dorm mother. She was firm and fair and at first a little awesome. She seemed to know a great deal about what went on in the hearts and minds of little boys. She was also a great story reader to lonely little boys and she gave a great scrub, even if you were the fifteenth dirty little kid in the bathtub lineup. Mr. Mitchell, our dorm father, was even more awesome than Mrs. Mitchell because he was very tall and had a scar on his chin.

In later years I learned that he was the only survivor of an explosion from an incendiary balloon bomb that the Japanese had floated over to the United States during World War II to set the forests on fire. At that time Archie Mitchell was a young pastor in Bly, Oregon. One day, he and his wife took a group of children on a Sunday school picnic in the woods. While he was unloading food from the car, the children discovered the unexploded bomb. Archie shouted a warning, but it was too late. A tree protected Archie from the blast and he survived. His first wife and all the children were killed in the explosion. They were the only civilians who died on the U.S. mainland during World War II as the result of hostile enemy action.

Mr. Mitchell had big, hard hands that were very gentle in the bathtub but unforgettable when applied to one's bottom. From the time I came to school until I was ten years old, I lived with the Mitchells in the dorm eight months out of every year. They provided a stability to dorm life that I liked. Living with them was very much like living with a favorite aunt and uncle.

I have already mentioned the Mitchells' oldest daughter, Rebecca. She was a tomboy. To the shame of all the boys, she could run faster and farther, jump and climb higher and play softball, basketball and just about every other game as well or better than any of us. She seemed to delight in proving that in every area she was better than the boys. The fact that her parents were the Mitchells made the situation particularly difficult. She made a great point of telling us that if we touched her, her father would squish any one of us "like a bug." It seemed totally plausible and naturally this did not endear her to us.

The Mitchells had three other children, all of whom I thought were nicer than Becki.

When I was eleven, the Mitchells returned to the United States. After one year of furlough, they tried to go back to South Vietnam, but the government refused to grant them visas until the following year. When they finally were able to return, the Mission assigned them to work in the city of Banmethuot in the central highlands. Becki enrolled in school as an ordinary missionary kid like the rest of us. She was still very athletic and as competitive as ever, but she no longer tormented us. In ninth grade I finally grew past her and as I matured physically and athletically she no longer posed a threat to my self-esteem. I liked girls to pay attention to me and did my best to impress them. Becki would not be impressed and so I ignored her—until one day when her father was kidnapped by the Viet Cong.

Mr. Mitchell was the director of the Leprosy Hospital about fifteen miles outside of Banmethuot. The staff included one missionary doctor, Dr. Ardel Vietti, and a number of other workers, including Dan Gerber, a young Mennonite agriculturalist. The Mitchell children had just arrived home for vacation when the first warnings of trouble came: three bridges leading to the leprosarium were burned by the Viet Cong. They also posted a warning against repairing the bridges. The missionaries, certain that the Viet Cong were not interested in them personally, continued their work at the leprosarium, fording the streams when they had to drive into Banmethuot.

On the evening of May 31, 1962 the Viet Cong struck again. As Mrs. Mitchell and the children watched in horror, the Viet Cong tied Mr. Mitchell's hands behind his back and marched him into the jungle, along with Dr. Vietti and Dan Gerber. No one ever saw or heard from any of them again.

The news of Mr. Mitchell's kidnapping shocked all of us. After all, if it could happen to Mr. Mitchell, it could happen to anyone's parents.

When the missionary kids returned to school a month later, we watched the Mitchell children with a sense of awe. They did not talk very much about their father. We never saw them crying, although I'm sure they did. Their lives went on as before, except that now they shared a common sorrow that bound them tightly together. I remember wondering how they could stand it day after day not knowing where their father might be or what he might be suffering. But I dared not ask. *What if it had been my father? Would he be locked up in a bamboo cage? Would he be tortured? Marched every day through the jungle? Chained in an underground Viet Cong cave?* The thought of it left me shaken and fearful. *How could they stand it?* It was a great mystery, one that I did not understand until many years later.

In 1965 I left Dalat School for the last time. I don't remember saying good-bye to the Mitchells. It seemed to me that in an indefinable way their experience had left them a cut above the rest of us. After the death of my own parents six years later, in that same city of Banmethuot, I learned that in the school of life, there is no better teacher than godly sorrow.

During my years at Geneva College I kept a sharp eye out for the right girl. I was certain that I would find her during college, since bachelorhood did not appeal to me. Finding the right girl, however, turned out to be more of a challenge than I had imagined. To begin with, I was still trying to figure out the American system of courtship. I was often perplexed. The social structure at Dalat School was designed to discourage kids who lived together from sunup to sundown from getting into serious romances. With such clearly defined goals, circumvention was a relatively simple matter. But my being an artist in manipulating the Dalat social system did not help at all in the United States.

During my senior high school year in America after several humiliating efforts at dating, I decided not to try anymore. But teenage hormones being what they are, my interest in girls soon overwhelmed my pride. By the time I graduated from high school I had dated most of the girls in my church's youth group. They probably were of the opinion that I was a nice fellow, but somewhat strange.

In college, however, the business of courtship became a serious matter since marriage was now a definite possibility. Mother had warned me to be very careful and had counseled me to ask the Lord to help me find the right girl. I determined to date only Christian girls, confident that I would recognize the right one when I saw her. Within a month I was going steady.

The courtship did not last long and was but the first in a series of short-lived romances bruising to both myself and the girls I dated. My problem was that if a girl wasn't a possibility for marriage, I wouldn't date her. If I started dating a girl and she dated someone else, I dropped her. It was all very intense. Once the girls found out how serious I was, they wanted to know a bit more about me. When they found out that I was planning to become a doctor, the friendship warmed up. When they found out that I was planning to be a missionary doctor, the relationship either cooled on the spot or gradually unraveled.

I became somewhat of a loner. After my parents' death, I didn't feel that I belonged to anyone anymore. Yes, I still had my brothers and sisters, but except for my sister Judy, we were separated by half a world. Judy and I got together every few months. We realized that if our family was to remain close we would have to take the initiative. The problem was that Dale, Laurel and Tom were still in Southeast Asia, having been willed to a missionary aunt and uncle, George and Harriet Irwin. The Irwins were not due to come home on furlough for three more years. Therefore, Judy and I decided that we would go to Vietnam. We had an intense longing to see where Mom and Dad had died and to see their grave.

As usual, we had no money, so we wrote to the Alliance leaders and begged them to help us with the tickets. We knew that sympathetic Christians had donated several thousand dollars to our Alliance Mission headquarters earmarked for the children of the martyred missionaries. The money was placed in a fund to pay for Dale, Laurel and Tom to go to college. Those who controlled the money did not feel that it was appropriate to use it to pay for our travel.

If we wanted to go to Vietnam, they said, we would have to pay our own way.

Their decision was bitterly disappointing. Actually, it took years for me to forgive them. I realize now that those who made the decision thought it was in our best interests, but the effects so splintered our family that it took considerable time and effort to repair the damage. My younger brother assumed that we did not care about him. Twelve long years later, during a belated family reunion, he shared how he had struggled with his anger toward us for our seeming indifference. The wounds are now healed, but I still dream of some day seeing my parents' grave.

But back to my courtship saga at Geneva College: an attractive girl planning a career in missionary medicine began to show an interest in me. I became so convinced that she was God's choice for me that I didn't bother to ask the Lord. Six months later she explained that I was not the right man for her. My world collapsed. In the pain of the moment, I turned to the Lord for companionship and love. Once again I found that when I hurt the most, God healed the best.

For the first time in my life I began to seriously consider celibacy. Previously the idea had repelled me, but now, still feeling like a boxer the day after losing a big fight, I was ready to think about it. In my heart I hoped I would still find the girl of my dreams, but now I was willing to just do nothing. If there was a right one, God would bring her to me. If there wasn't, I could wait, perhaps forever.

Two months later I rediscovered Becki Mitchell!

I was attending summer school and had already been accepted to the University of Pittsburgh School of Medicine for the fall semester of 1969. Because my younger brother Dale was returning to the States from Dalat School, I drove to New York to meet him. At my sister's house in Nyack I learned that one of my former classmates in Malaysia was getting married in a few weeks. We were all invited to a Dalat reunion party at the home of a retired missionary.

As far as parties go, it was pretty tame. The room was crowded, and after loading up my plate with cookies I sat down in a corner to talk with some old friends. About half an hour into the evening I noticed a very attractive brunette sitting across the room. I thought, *This is supposed to be a Dalat school reunion, but I don't recognize that girl.* I leaned over to my sister.

"Who is that nice-looking girl?" I whispered.

When she told me that it was Becki Mitchell, I laughed right out loud. A second look assured me that indeed it was Becki. What a difference five years had made!

She noticed me staring at her. I moved to the other side of the room and introduced myself. To my surprise she was friendly and even remembered me! As we talked, I learned that despite all the years we had gone to Dalat school together, I really did not know her at all. She had opinions, intelligence and a charm that left me feeling warm all over! Forgotten were the days when she out-ran, out-jumped, out-climbed and outplayed me. When it was time to go home I regretfully said good night.

"It just doesn't seem fair," I complained to my sister as we got into the car. "The most interesting girl I've met in years goes to school in Tacoma, Washington while I go to school in Pittsburgh!" There was clearly no future in that.

I drove back to Pittsburgh with my brother, a maze of conflicting emotions running rampant through my mind. All week long I prayed about Becki Mitchell, asking the Lord to show me what to do next. By the end of the week I knew what I had to do: pursue her!

The following weekend I decided I should visit my sister again in Nyack. Surely my brother Dale needed to see more of his sister—it seemed only natural! After a nine-hour drive we arrived at 2 a.m. At 8 a.m. the next morning I dialed Becki's number. To my surprise she agreed to go out with me that night.

It was the beginning of a special friendship and a great romance. Having both lost missionary parents, Becki and I understood each other's feelings almost intuitively. We had both struggled, vainly trying to understand God's purpose and both of us had finally ended up holding on to the admonition of Proverbs 3:5: "Trust in the LORD with all your heart and lean not on your own understanding." We had both learned that absolute trust in God does not preclude emotional suffering. Finally, we both had experienced a kind of unconfirmable loss—the ones we had loved were gone, but we had never personally seen the irrefutable evidence of their deaths. My parents and her dad had just sort of disappeared. The only difference was that I knew my parents were in heaven, while she still did not know if her father was dead or alive. As we shared our feelings, the powerful magnetism of common suffering bound us together. It became pure pleasure to drive eight hours—and pay the tolls—every weekend on the Pennsylvania Turnpike.

In September we left for opposite ends of the North American continent: Becki to continue her nurse's training in Tacoma and I to begin medical school in Pittsburgh. During Christmas break I had ten days off. A friend of mine wanted to go to California for the break, so we agreed to take his car and share the driving. I was put in charge of the food for the trip and since bologna was cheap, I made forty bologna sandwiches.

As soon as classes were out we started off, changing drivers every two hours. Instead of stopping to eat, we ate the bologna sandwiches I had prepared. At first they tasted pretty good, but by the second day we couldn't stand them. We reached Sacramento, California in forty-eight hours. Becki met me there with her aunt's car and we drove through beautiful snow-covered forests to Klamath Falls, Oregon to spend the holidays with her aunt and uncle.

Within two weeks of that first meeting in Nyack, I knew that I wanted to marry her. I was madly in love with her and I thought she loved me; but would she marry me? It seemed a bit rash to ask so soon. What if she turned me down? What would I do then? It was a thought more terrifying than death.

Becki welcomed me so enthusiastically in Sacramento that I took heart. Two days after Christmas and the day before I had to leave, we climbed a hill overlooking Klamath Falls. Snowflakes were drifting down, camouflaging the city lights below in an almost make-believe glow. Alone on the hill, two people embraced. One was enjoying the romantic moment; one was terrified. I was at a crossroads in my life and this girl had the power to crush me or to make me intoxicatingly happy. The only sound in that silent night was our breathing. I stopped breathing and asked her to marry me.

I had expected her to stop breathing too, either in shock or astonishment. Surely she would at least want to think about it for an hour or so. She might even want to think—no, pray—about it for a week. When she answered "yes" in the next breath, I nearly fainted.

"Are you sure?" I asked. "I mean, really?" I couldn't believe I had heard right. She was laughing at me. Of course she was sure! She had been sure of it since the night of the Dalat reunion in Nyack. That same night she had gone home and written her mother that she had met the man she was going to marry. She had been waiting for me the whole time!

After so many disappointments, I was afraid to believe that God could be so good to me. As the months passed and the letters and phone calls confirmed that her love for me was real, I began to see more clearly a side of God I had forgotten—His benevolence. I had seen Him surround His deeds in clouds of impenetrable mystery and I had heard Him demand trust and obedience. Now His goodness, love and kindness unfolded like the petals of a flower in bloom. He had miraculously provided for all of my financial needs. He had opened the high and forbidding gates to medical school and now He had given me the bright promise that I would once again belong to someone.

On June 26, 1971 Becki and I were married.

From *On Call* by David C. Thompson, M.D. © 1991 by Christian Publications, Inc.

Dr. David Thompson was born in Pittsburgh, Pennsylvania in 1948. When he was four months old, his parents left the U.S. to serve as missionaries in Cambodia, taking their baby with them. In 1966 they were reassigned to Vietnam, where both his parents were killed by North Vietnamese soldiers. This event severely tested his faith and forced him to choose between a life of bitterness or a life of trust in God. He chose the latter. After he finished medical school and became a doctor, he and his wife, Becki, expected to return to Southeast Asia. Instead, they were assigned to head up a medical missionary team in Gabon, a small and mostly primitive country on the west coast of equatorial Africa. The Thompsons served twenty two years at that location. In August 2000, after furlough, they went back for another four-year term in Gabon. Their experiences on the mission field are described in riveting detail in *On Call*, from which this story is taken.

Confronting in Love

Florence Littauer

*A*ll of us like stories that have happy endings. Women love to see Cinderella marry Prince Charming, ride off into the sunset, buy a big castle with a moat and raise adorable little children and fluffy little dogs. Men dream of business and financial success and some hope to be athletic heroes.

Fred and I were typical. We really thought we could get married and live happily ever after, but right from the start we found we were nothing alike and didn't see eye to eye on anything. We didn't think our church backgrounds would make much difference, but we couldn't agree on a mutual denomination. We found out our personalities didn't match; I wanted fun and he wanted things perfect. We thought we'd have adorable children who'd grow up to be brilliant and successful, but we lost our two longed-for sons. I thought Fred would make lots of money and we'd live in lavish houses. Sometimes he did and sometimes we did. But sometimes we didn't. Our whole life story could be charted out in the ups and downs of houses.

When we committed our lives to the Lord Jesus we thought, *This is the answer. Now we'll be happy.* The adoption of Freddie certainly should have cheered us up. But I had operations, depression, disappointments. We moved to the desert of California to go into full-time Christian service. Surely God would bless such dedication, but after losing money on our Connecticut home and putting money into Bungalow One at Arrowhead Springs, we were forced to leave it all and move on.

We built a big house in the foothills above San Bernardino and entertained the saints. I pictured living in that home forever, that home the Lord protected from the fire; but with financial problems and a call from the Lord we sold the dream and moved to a tiny condominium. We started CLASS (Christian Leaders, Authors and Speakers Seminars). We moved to a normal house. I wrote seventeen books and spoke all over the country. Did we finally get to Happy Ever After time? Were the tough times over? I thought so.

Throughout our married life I had little to do with Fred's businesses. I had married him expecting financial security and yet through all our years we had never really reached it. We'd had many good years, but then something would happen and Fred's plans would fail. He always had logical excuses and I had no choice but to believe him.

He was always optimistic and couldn't see why a loss of money bothered me. "It's only money," he'd say. He never understood that because I had grown up poor and I had a desperate desire to be financially secure. I didn't need to be rich; I just needed to know the bills were paid.

As my speaking and writing ministry grew, I had even less to do with Fred's business. He always led me to believe things were going well until I came home from one weekend retreat to find we'd had some major financial losses and some legal entanglements. There was no dishonesty or malicious intent, but the situation was upsetting and humiliating.

My daughter Marita and I discussed what we should do about Fred's apparent inability to succeed for any length of time. We were also concerned about the anger he seemed to have pent up inside him. I had never really thought of him as angry before because he never yelled or hit me. Yet as Marita and I talked over the situation, I realized that the reason he didn't display his anger was that I had learned to avoid triggering it. As long as I was supportive and submissive, he didn't get mad. If I questioned his decisions or directions, he'd give me what I called "The Look," a flash from his eyes that said, "I dare you." I never dared.

Because Fred had always been a loving husband—polite, gracious and generous—I had denied or ignored any recognition of deep-seated problems in his life. But this financial and legal turmoil brought up feelings I didn't know I had.

I tried to tell Fred that I felt he had some hurts in his past he hadn't dealt with, but he flatly denied it. When I suggested I felt he had an odd relationship with his mother, he angrily defended her and said sternly to me, "Don't you ever say a bad thing about my mother."

I continued trying different approaches to make him realize the source of what I felt was a long-range problem, not just the financial crisis of the moment.

He could not see that his repeated business difficulties were anything more than occasional bad luck.

When I felt I was getting nowhere, Marita and I decided we needed a time of confrontation. With our friend and counselor Lana Bateman as the outside, objective party, we asked to speak with Fred about a serious matter. When we told him we saw a lot of anger inside him, he denied it—and got angry. As we enumerated examples, he began to listen and suddenly his reaction softened and he agreed to see a male counselor we had already consulted. In the interim we were functioning as usual.

One day as we were waiting to appear on the PTL Club with Gary McSpadden, we turned on the television monitor to see Becky Tirabassi. Becky has a testimony of teenage alcoholism. She pledged to the Lord that if He would save her, she'd spend at least one hour a day in written prayer. As Fred watched her story, the Lord convicted him that he should write his prayers and he began the next day.

During the three months before he went for his two weeks of intensive therapy, Fred wrote out his prayers each day. By the time he got to the counseling he was ready for God to do a great work.

In counseling, Fred learned that he was a victim of rejection by both his mother and father. They were always working and never came to any of his sporting events or performances. Instead of encouraging young Fred, his mother had, in fact, told him he'd never succeed at anything. Little did we understand at the time that Fred's inability to stay on top for long was a fulfillment of that prophecy of doom.

He also learned that his mother had a lot of anger in her that spilled out on Fred as a child. He was always made to say he was sorry even when the situation was not his fault. He'd stuffed his anger inside him because he couldn't vent it on her. As we look back now, he had unconsciously done the same with me. Whatever the problem, I had to apologize. After a while I had learned to do it without feeling, as a cheap price for peace.

When Fred told the therapist that after his father's death his mother had moved him into her bedroom and made him her new husband in every way but sexually, the counselor explained this was an emotional form of sexual abuse.

Fred did not come home healed; instead, he was confused, introspective and remote. He had done what we'd asked him to do and he felt worse. He continued his written prayer, began to read everything he could on rejection and abuse, and spent hours in Bible study seeking God's answers for his life. Gradually we saw changes: "The Look" was gone and there was a new peace in his demeanor. As Marita and I saw the difference, we encouraged him. The Lord began to bring people to him who had hidden their pains of the past and couldn't figure out why they were angry. As Fred helped others, he developed steps that God used to heal him and those he counseled.

So much happened so quickly. As Fred became vulnerable and willing to share and as the Lord used him to help others, he felt strongly led to write *Freeing Your Mind from Memories That Bind.* He had never written before and really had never planned to, but as he says now, that was because he had nothing to say. Now he does.

The Lord has given him a special gift for uncovering the root of people's problems and filling in the gaps in their memories. We have learned that until someone finds out the cause of their problems (the source of the pain), the symptoms don't go away. The Lord only heals what we bring to Him.

The Lord showed Fred that he should get out of business ventures and trust that we could support ourselves in speaking, writing and ministering to others. With the Lord's blessing this has become possible. Now as we travel full-time together, being home only a few days a month, we have learned to love each other in a new dimension and feel as if we are on a perpetual honeymoon. We've faced our problems squarely. We've sought the Lord's wisdom and He has helped us to make the tough times count.

> From *I've Found My Keys, Now Where's My Car?*
> by Florence Littauer, copyright © 1994 by Florence Littauer. Published by Thomas Nelson Publishers. Used by permission of the author.

 Florence Littauer, founder of CLASS (Christian Leaders, Authors and Speakers Seminars, Inc.) is author of over twenty-six books, many of them best-sellers in the Christian market. With her husband, Fred, she travels nationally and internationally as a Christian speaker, sharing her humor and valuable insights. Her latest book, *Understanding Your*

Child's Personality, was written in response to numerous requests from those who had heard her speak and read her other books on personality types. She is a frequent keynote speaker for retreats, business conferences and seminars.

E-mail: SLVRBX@aol.com

Set Free from the Past

Lloyd John Ogilvie

*J*he power of Christ to heal memories and set people free from the past is exemplified in what He did for a couple in our congregation. I've been given permission to tell this story. The couple involved wants it known. What happened to them, they yearn to have happen to other couples. Their very exciting healing occurred as a result of experiencing the power of forgiveness.

I remember when I first heard about them. Their physician called me. He said that he and the psychiatrist needed my help. The husband was in the hospital, very ill with a serious case of ulcers. His stomach was being eaten out as a result of worry. The doctor said, "We need to get together. As we understand it, the real problem is that this man's wife will not forgive him of an infraction of their marital vows. As a result, she feels that she must judge him and keep him at arm's length."

The five of us—the internist and the psychiatrist, the couple and I—gathered together. We talked over the situation. I realized that deeper counseling was going to be necessary for the wife. She felt so righteous in her indignation. She had taken vengeance into her own hands and felt called to punish her husband for what he had done. Her attitude toward him was aloof, cold and negative. As a result she allowed no affection between them and constantly reminded him of what he had done to hurt her. His appeals for forgiveness and a new chance were rejected. At the same time she did not believe in divorce and was determined to live the rest of her life with the sword of hostility drawn.

Later, after a long time of listening and caring as the wife and I talked alone, I said, "Dear friend, have you ever failed in your own sexual life?"

Her face drained of blood. She became white. She said, "Why did you ask that question? You have no right to ask that question! What does that have to do with my inability to forgive my husband?"

Persisting, I said, "Just tell me. Was there ever a time when you failed, either in attitude or in action?"

Then, tumbling out of her heart, came the story of a failure in her teenage years, with an older man, and all the problems that had resulted. She'd covered it up. Thought no one knew. Kept it from her parents and her friends, the memory guarded deep down inside her. Her unforgiving memory had caused her to deal with her husband's failure with such terrible indignation and vengeance.

The woman seemed relieved that at least one person knew about her secret. When she felt reassured of my confidentiality, she talked about it freely, relating the guilt and anguish the memory had caused her.

When the timing was right, I asked, "Could it be that your guilt over what you have done has made it especially difficult to forgive your husband? Is there an interrelationship between your inability to accept forgiveness and forgive yourself, and your refusal to forgive your husband?"

As we talked further she realized that her husband's failure had forced her to relive her own. What she had been doing to him she really felt *she* had deserved. Yet since no one knew, she had felt she was left to be her own judge. Her childhood conditioning in the Christian faith had been focused on rules and regulations. There had been little or no teaching or experience in forgiveness. And what she had done was, in her mind, the one thing God would never forgive. She had suppressed her feelings all through the years. Then, when she learned of her husband's mistake, she let them fly with a vengeance.

I shared with this distraught wife the truth of Scripture about Christ's forgiveness and unconditional love. Then we talked about His power to heal memories. The Lord blessed the conversation, creating a willingness in the woman to let go of her false idea about His condemnation and releasing her to consider the truth of His compassion.

Her reverence for the Bible was a dynamic plus. We went through passage after passage about grace. Finally she was ready to surrender her hurting memory for Christ's healing. We prayed together, accepting the Lord's forgiveness for her.

In a subsequent visit, we focused on the implications of her healed memory for her forgiveness for her husband. She related how her feelings about him had mysteriously changed since she felt healed of the past. A new tenderness and warmth began to grow in her. We talked through how she could communicate forgiveness to her husband in words, actions and attitudes. She pictured the actual way and words that she would use.

Again we prayed. Then she left my office to go to the hospital to be a channel of Christ's love for her husband. It worked. She told him about her own experience of healing and expressed tender forgiveness.

In the weeks that followed, the husband began to recover. He responded readily to treatment and soon was able to go home. Nourished by the new relationship between him and his wife, he was able to return to work long before the doctors had expected.

The man's experience of his wife's forgiveness was only the beginning of a spiritual pilgrimage still ahead of him. He still needed to accept the Lord's forgiveness. I saw him in church each week, listening intently. Then one Sunday my heart leaped with joy as I saw him come down the aisle and pray with one of the elders. He claimed the Lord's forgiveness for his failure and asked for the healing of his memory.

Some weeks later both the husband and wife came forward for prayer. Afterward they exclaimed, "That was more than a healing service at the end of this morning's service. For us it was a remarriage service!"

And so it was. Christ, the healing power of the world, had healed their individual memories and had made them one again. His words sounded in my soul as I looked into their radiant faces: "Neither do I condemn you" (John 8:11). Then my heart sang with Paul's words, "Therefore, there is now no condemnation for those who are in Christ Jesus" (Romans 8:1).

And so it happens. Christ is the healer of memories for all of us. We are prompted to ask, "What memories does He long to heal in me?" Tell Him all about it. Then He will help you receive what has been yours all along: forgiveness and the power to forgive.

From *Why Not Accept God's Healing and Wholeness?* by Lloyd John Ogilvie. Copyright © Fleming H. Revell, a division of Baker Book House. Reprinted by permission.

Dr. Lloyd John Ogilvie is Chaplain of the United States Senate; he was for many years Senior Pastor of the historic First Presbyterian Church of Hollywood, California. He frequently speaks at conferences and universities and is author of over thirty-seven books, recently including *Acts of the Holy Spirit* and *Facing the Future Without Fear*. His radio and television ministry, *Let God Love You*, touched millions of people across the nation. He combines a rich blend of scholarship and fresh inspiration with real-life stories about the great adventure of life in Christ.

Back from the Brink

Kris Erickson

While attending a Christian college in southern California, I met a young man with dark brown hair, blue eyes and an adventurous spirit. When his dorm room was too noisy, he found a balcony and slept hanging in a three-point suspension hammock he had designed. He drew funny cartoons showing every aspect of campus life, all on one page. In geology class field trips, things that scared everyone else, like rappelling backward off an overhanging rock to study rock formations, exhilarated him.

I admired Michael's many talents. I had the opportunity to climb Mount Rainier with him while working in Washington state one summer. We talked of hopes and dreams, and found we had a lot in common. But I had grown up in an abusive home and had little confidence. I figured I'd have no chance to know him well.

Our paths parted, but though he stayed in Washington state and I returned to southern California, we wrote many long letters. After I graduated from college, I moved to Washington state and we were married.

I tried at first to hide my past from him. I thought he would think less of me once he knew I was really a frightened person trying to function, and to heal, in a fast-paced world. My confidence had been so severely damaged that sometimes even normal tasks seemed overwhelming.

I was in trouble right after I moved to Washington state. Though I had managed to get a California driver's license, I had to retake the driver's test to get a Washington license. The move had brought so many changes to my life that when I found out about the test, I was horrified to hear my voice shrieking out of control,

"I can't do it! I can't!"

All the while I was thinking: *Now I've blown it. Michael will see the real me and know he's in over his head.*

Michael didn't react negatively. "It's all right," he said simply. "You're under a lot of stress. I'll drive for you, for now."

His straightforward answer eased my panic. My family had overreacted at even small challenges, so I had learned to overreact rather than face things one step at a time. Michael's calm reaction helped put my feelings into perspective. When I told him why I was so scared, I got a huge shock.

"My past wasn't perfect either," he said.

He went on to explain how he had been beaten as an infant, how his parents' messy divorce landed him and his brother in a foster home for almost a year, and how, when his mother remarried, his stepfather's constant moves kept him so off balance, academically, he never finished high school.

"How did you learn to draw, climb mountains and create things like your hammock?" I asked. I had been beaten for nearly eighteen years and had my confidence shredded by constant verbal abuse. Though I made it through high school and college, I left no lasting impressions in people's minds.

"There were times I didn't have many choices," Michael explained. "But I learned to focus on what I could do, not what I couldn't do. When I was a little kid in Alaska, we had no electricity. I sat under the kitchen table with a candle and drew. When my stepfather changed jobs, I found mountains to climb."

I hugged him, then sighed, still frustrated. "I never did anything right in my mom's eyes. When I tried to do as you did, she would take away whatever I found to do."

He hugged me back and said, "Your mom isn't here now."

He was right. My mom had died of cancer many years before. As I relaxed, he whispered in my ear, "God won't give us anything we can't handle if we look to Him as our partner."

"Can we start over again, right now?" I answered. "Next time I think something is too hard, remind me to look for what I *can* do, and do at least that much. I'll look to God to help me do more."

That's what we've been doing for the past fourteen years. We aren't rich or famous, but Michael has a good job as a concept artist, and I am a loving mother, freelance writer and composer. I overcame my fear and got a driver's license. We still have mountains in our lives, but we choose to keep climbing, one step at a time, with God as our partner. One step at a time.

Kris Erickson is a freelance writer with over 100 stories, articles, devotionals, a cheesecake cookbook and the first book of a fantasy series published to date. She was born in Butler, New Jersey, and has a Bachelor of Arts degree in Theology from Ambassador College. Kris is married to concept cartoonist Michael Erickson. They live in Bonny Lake, Washington and have a six-year-old son, Jason.

E-mail: slverkriss@aol.com

Healing Marriages through Prayer

Tim LaHaye

A frantic call came from a distraught mother in Tucson, Arizona. "My son Rick and his wife Jan live there in San Diego and are going to file for divorce on Thursday, but they promised to see a minister if I found one who would counsel them. My pastor knows you and has read all your books. He said you would meet with them."

To be very honest, my counseling load at the time was about to drown me; I didn't need any out-of-state additions. But before I could say no, this deeply burdened mother added the magic words, "They have three children." No Christian counselor I know could turn down an opportunity like that.

When they arrived on Tuesday night, they were obviously just fulfilling an obligation to Rick's mother before destroying a marriage of thirteen years. Rick started by saying, "Pastor, forgive us for wasting your time. There is nothing that can save this marriage." To prove his point he continued, "We have been to a

Christian counseling center in Los Angeles. The counselor gave us a battery of psychological tests and found that we were so hopelessly mismatched that we ought to get a divorce!" Suddenly my juices began pumping, for whoever came to that conclusion did not understand the power of God. Then Rick gave me the best lead-in I've ever had: "What do you think of that advice?"

I replied, "What I think about it is really not important." (I didn't want to tell them it was the worst advice I had ever heard.) "But you do need to hear what God says about it." Turning to First Corinthians 7:10, 27, I read these words: "Now to the married I command, yet not I but the Lord: A wife is not to depart from her husband. . . . Are you bound to a wife? Do not seek to be loosed" (NKJV). I shall never forget Rick's response. With a sneer on his face he challenged, "You mean God wants us to be this miserable the rest of our lives?"

"No," I explained, "God wants you to be happy the rest of your lives, but it will never come by disobeying His precepts. Since God is the author of marriage, He intended it to be the most sublime relationship two people can share on this earth." They could not experience the joy of marriage, even though they were Christians, because they were selfishly disobeying several of God's basic principles.

Fortunately for their children, those two parents got down on their knees with me and resurrendered their wills to God. They admitted their sins—he of selfish anger, she of selfish fears—and today they enjoy a model relationship.

While we were on our knees I suddenly realized that we had come to a position of new beginnings, and I have used this approach many times since. Many couples enter into marriage on their knees before God. As soon as the minister pronounces the couple man and wife, he leads them to kneel at the prayer bench or the altar as an act of humble submission, followed by a prayer that invokes God's blessings on their brand-new home and relationship. But very honestly, happiness in marriage is based not on the minister's prayer but on your continued acts of compliance with the will of God.

Every person and almost every marriage will face a crisis point when one or both people think they cannot endure the conflict, disagreement and pressure one moment longer. But instead of flying into a rage and aggravating each other, they must learn to surrender the problem, their lives and their wills to God.

My wife and I are both strong-willed people. If I said we agreed on everything, I would be lying. It would be closer to the truth to admit that we disagree on almost everything—except those issues for which we have already established guidelines.

If there are two ways to do something or go somewhere, she will choose one and I the other. Yet we enjoy a fabulous relationship. Why? Because differences never cause us to lose respect for each other. We even respectfully recognize the right of our partner to be wrong. We have also learned to pray about our differences. When Bev prefers one pathway and I have made a different choice, we have learned to commit our difference to God.

After conducting over seven hundred Family Life seminars for close to a million people during these last twenty-six years, I have received one comment consistently: "The principle we learned from your seminar that helped our marriage most was your instruction on 'couple prayer.' "

Couple prayer is a form of conversational prayer with your partner. The ground rules are very simple. On the first night the husband should lead, praying for the initial burden on his heart for thirty seconds to two minutes, after which he stops. His pause allows his wife to provide an addendum, praying briefly for that same burden. When she finishes, she too just stops. At that point the husband introduces the second burden on his heart, after which the wife responds in kind. Each time she will address the issue from her perspective, addressing God in ways that did not occur to him. We have discovered that we often share concerns during prayer times that we forget to discuss on the conscious level.

I know nothing that will grind off differences between partners or bind two people together better than couple prayer. Remember the couple that came to my office on Tuesday night before seeing the attorney? They were the first couple I introduced to this kind of couple prayer, thirty years ago. Couple prayer for them was a lifesaver, not only enriching their relationship but rescuing their marriage.

Try it. It will enhance your capacity to love and become best friends—even if you are total opposites.

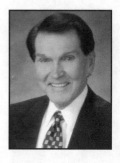

Dr. Tim LaHaye is a noted author, minister and nationally recognized speaker on Bible prophecy. He holds a doctor of ministry degree from Western Theological Seminary and a doctor of literature degree from Liberty University. For twenty-five years he pastored one of the nation's outstanding churches in San Diego and founded two Christian high schools, a Christian school system of ten schools and Christian Heritage College. He is founder of both Tim LaHaye Ministries and The Pre-Trib Research Center. Dr. LaHaye has written over forty books, with over 22 million copies in print in thirty-three languages. His current fiction works, written with Jerry B. Jenkins (the *Left Behind* series), have all been at the top of the Christian best-seller charts.

Does God Care?

Catherine Marshall

*I*t was sometime during my teens that I received my first clear shaft of light on the riddle of evil. There was growing larger and larger in my mind the contrast between my loving, compassionate parents and a God who allowed terrible things to happen. One day I took this puzzling question to a woman who had become a very special friend.

Mrs. MacDonald was one of those remarkable people who love all young people. Because she never talked down to teenagers, many of us gave her our complete confidence. She was married to a Scotsman, a successful lawyer. On occasions when he had to be away from home on law cases, I would spend the night with her. Those evenings were talkfests.

The flavor of Mrs. Mac's life was reflected in her home. Windows were filled with African violets. On the stair landing stood a grandfather clock whose musical chimes marked the quarter-hours. There were current books of history and travel lying about. Just before bedtime Mrs. Mac and I would always have heaping bowls of ice cream—more ice cream than I could eat. Then she would tuck me under an eiderdown in a mahogany bed with tall pineapple posts.

On one of these evenings I found myself spilling out my inner rebellion against a God who permitted suffering and evil when He had the power to stop it.

"Catherine," she said thoughtfully, "you know how often I speak of Kenneth?"

I nodded. Quickly my mind reviewed what I knew about Kenneth. He had been the MacDonalds' only son, who had died of diabetes as a teenager. It had compounded their sorrow that insulin had been discovered just a few months too late to save their boy. Here then, close at home, was an example of the kind of tragedy that made me question the love of God.

"Well," my friend went on, "if I had reasoned as you suggest, I could have railed bitterly against God for allowing Kenneth's death. God has power. He could have prevented it, so why didn't He?

"Even now, I can't give you a complete answer to that. But I can't be bitter either, because during Kenneth's long illness, I had so many examples of God's tender father-love. Like that time soon after Kenneth himself suspected that he was going to die and asked me, 'Mother, what is it like to die? Mother, does it hurt?' "

Even as Mrs. Mac repeated the questions, tears sprang to my eyes, "How—did you answer him?"

The white-haired woman seemed to be seeing into the past. "I remember that I fled to the kitchen, supposedly to attend to something on the stove. I leaned against the kitchen cabinet. Queer, I'll never forget certain tiny details, like the feel of my knuckles pressed hard against the smooth, cold surface. And I asked God how to answer my boy.

"God did tell me. Only He could have given me the answer to the hardest question that a mother can ever be asked. I knew—just knew how to explain death to him. 'Kenneth,' I remember saying, 'you know how when you were a tiny boy, you used to play so hard all day that when night came, you would be too tired to undress—so you would tumble into Mother's bed and fall asleep?

" 'That was not your bed. It was not where you belonged. And you would only stay there a little while. In the morning—to your surprise—you would wake up and find yourself in your own bed in your own room. You were there because someone had loved you and had taken care of you. Your father had come—with his great strong arms—and carried you away.'

"So I told Kenneth that death is like that. We just wake up some morning to find ourselves in another room—our own room, where we belong. We shall be there, because God loves us even more than our human fathers and takes care of us just as tenderly."

We were both silent for a moment. Then Mrs. Mac said softly, "Kenneth never had any fear of dying after that. If—for some reason that I still don't understand—he could not be healed, then this taking away of all fear was the next greatest gift God could give us. And in the end, Kenneth went on into the next life exactly as God had told me he would—gently, sweetly." There was the look of profound peace on my friend's face as she spoke.

After Mrs. Mac tucked me in that night, I lay in the mahogany bed under the eiderdown, pondering her words. What she had really been telling me was that those on the inside of tragedy are often initiated into something that outsiders may not experience at all: the love of God—instant, continuous, real—in the midst of their trouble. With the presence of the Giver, they have something more precious than any gift He might bestow.

Not until years later, after my marriage to Peter Marshall, did I experience this for myself. During our first happy year in Atlanta, we had a close friend who had known much trouble—the death of children, financial reverses, the misunderstanding of friends. She used to look quizzically at us—young, so in love, fresh in our faith in the goodness of God.

"Neither of you has really had any trouble," she would say. "You're bound to have some sooner or later. Everyone does. When trouble comes to you, I wonder if you will feel as you do now?"

That friend's prediction was right. We did have trouble—much illness, and finally Peter Marshall's death at forty-six. So now I am in a better position to answer the friend's question. The answer is yes, I still believe in God's love, believe more firmly than ever, because my faith has stood trial.

A few hours before Peter's death I found out what the Hebrew poet meant when he wrote about "the everlasting arms" (Deuteronomy 33:27). I experienced the comfort of those arms. It happened in the early morning hours after Peter had been taken by ambulance to the hospital. I was forced to stay behind so that our young son Peter John would not be in the house alone.

There was no doubt that Peter's life hung in the balance. I sank to the floor by the bed, put my head in my arms, pondering how should I pray. Suddenly there was the feeling of being surrounded by the love of God the Father—enveloped in it, cradled with infinite gentleness.

Awe swept through me, followed by the conviction that it was not necessary to ask for anything. All I had to do was to commit Peter and me and our future to this great love. At the time I thought this meant that Peter's heart would be healed.

Much later—when I had trodden the long way through the Valley of the Shadow—I realized that God had given me this experience in the hours preceding Peter's death so that I might have absolute assurance that He was beside Peter and me every minute, loving us, sharing Peter's glory and my grief.

That is how I came to know personally that the Apostle Paul's glowing assertion is literally true: that nothing—neither death, nor life, nor tribulation, nor peril of any sort shall be able to separate us from the love of God. (See Romans 8:35-39.)

Then, in the years that followed Peter Marshall's death, I thought I glimpsed another shaft of light illuminating the dark night of human sorrow. Not only is God always beside us in trouble, identified with our suffering, but He can also make everything—even our troubles and sorrows—"work together for good" (Romans 8:28, KJV).

Many times I have received letters from readers whom I have never met, who marveled at how God accomplished this in our case . . . "How I wish that I might have heard Dr. Marshall preach! But so far away here in New Zealand, I would never have known about him at all, had it not been for *A Man Called Peter*. And now, to think that he is preaching [through this book] to more people than ever today."

This is not to say that God willed Peter's death in order that He might bring about a widened ministry. Rather that given his death, God could turn even that to good.

From *Beyond Ourselves* by Catherine Marshall. Original Copyright 1961 by Catherine Marshall; Current Publisher is Baker Book House, Grand Rapids, MI.

Catherine Marshall authored several books that are considered classics: *A Man Called Peter* (her husband's biography) and *Beyond Ourselves* are two examples. Her best-selling novel, *Christy*, became the basis for a TV series by the same title. Catherine Marshall died in 1983, but her books are still in demand and probably will be for generations to come.

Section 4

Children

Train a child in the way he should go,
and when he is old he will not turn from it.
(Proverbs 22:6)

When Strings Turn to Wings

David Jeremiah

*I*t seems like only yesterday that I hugged and kissed my nineteen-year-old Jennifer just before she stepped onto a USAir 767 taking her back to Dayton, Ohio and the third quarter of her freshman year at Cedarville College.

Moments later I put my arms around my older son, David, and held him to me for a while before I hugged and kissed his beautiful wife, Cami, and watched them walk off toward the American Airlines corridor and their flight back home to Raleigh, North Carolina.

Seven of us suddenly had become four.

We headed back to San Diego and later that afternoon drove to Coronado, where I dropped off my older daughter, Jan, and hugged and kissed her outside the door to the apartment she then called "home."

And then we were down to three.

For seven straight nights, all seven of us had eaten dinner together at the same table at the same time in the same place. Neither Donna nor I could remember when that had last occurred—even when we all lived in the same house. What a memory-making week for the Jeremiah family, a precious, joyous gift of one whole week spent with those who are the dearest to us on this earth!

In many ways, it seemed as if we had never been apart. I think it's like that for families who are close. There is no period of adjustment, no getting used to each other. It's as if we picked up the conversations where we last left them. But by Saturday the conversations ended and we split three ways to get back to "normal."

Did I say "normal"?

That was normal then; these days our home is down to two. Daniel, our youngest, is now a sophomore at Appalachian State University, clear across a wide continent in Boone, North Carolina. And Donna and I feel the empty-nest syndrome in full force. I think that part of the sadness of our children leaving home is the realization that we are growing older.

Jan was the first of ours to leave home. I remember taking her to Schroon Lake, New York, where she was enrolled at Word of Life Bible Institute. We went there together, just the two of us, and stayed in an old cabin by the lake. Everything seemed cold and dark. If you live in California, as I do, you forget how overcast the skies can grow back east. You forget how heavy and leaden that can feel. That day was dreary, dark and sad, and that night I didn't sleep much.

We got up early the next morning and walked to registration, held in a huge gymnasium loaded with tables festooned with tall signs and manned by total strangers. I asked my daughter, "Do you want me to go through registration with you?"

"I think I can do it myself." she replied. And so she did.

Later we met for lunch. And all too soon it was time for me to go. I climbed in my rental car and drove ninety miles back down the mountain to the Albany airport, silent and alone. I came home without my daughter. I'm not ashamed to admit it was a terribly sad journey.

It was 4 o'clock in the morning when David left. If you're not going to sleep all night, I suppose you might as well get up at 4 o'clock. He and David Beezer, his good buddy, packed all their stuff in the back of our David's Ford Ranger truck, threw a tarp over everything and tied it down, then headed off twenty-seven hundred miles to Liberty University in Lynchburg, Virginia to play football.

And I stood in the driveway at 4 a.m. and sobbed like a baby.

The year Jennifer left for school I took her and her mother to Lindbergh Field to get on a plane. They were going a week early so they could buy winter clothes in a place where such necessities didn't cost as much as they do in San Diego. Donna was going to help her get settled in the dorm and ready for school. So the two of them boarded the plane . . . and left me standing there, all by myself. I came home and realized that life was really changing for the Jeremiah family. Strings were turning to wings.

When our kids come home for a visit, we want them to feel they're really home, not staying in some faceless hotel. We don't treat their rooms as holy shrines or as untouchable memorials stuck in a time-warp of parental nostalgia, but we do want our kids to know they're still a part of our family, even though they may be living far away with families of their own.

We love it when our children visit and we covet our time with them. It's so good to be a family!

Even when strings turn to wings, our relationship as parent-to-children remains intact. We never stop being Mom and Dad, and they never stop being Son or Daughter.

I hope that no matter what trouble any of my children might fall into, they'll always know that somewhere is a father who loves them. A father who will love them as he's been loved by his Father in heaven.

Our Heavenly Father loves us unconditionally. He's the God of a hundred million chances who is always there to encourage and strengthen us. I'd like to believe that will be the goal for all of us when strings turn to wings.

Dr. David Jeremiah is a pastor, author, conference speaker and radio/ television minister. His "Turning Point" radio programs are heard on over 900 stations across the country. He has written ten books and is a regular guest speaker at Moody Pastor's Conference and other prestigious colleges and conferences. He is senior pastor at Shadow Mountain

Community Church in San Diego,
CA and Chancellor of Christian Heritage College.

Contact: Dr. David Jeremiah
P.O. Box 3838
San Diego, CA 92163

Website: www.turningpointradio.org

My Miracle Tape

Barbara Johnson

*9*n the afternoon of August 1, 1973, my son, Tim, called me from Whitehorse, in the Yukon Territory of northwestern Canada. He was on the way home after spending the summer with his friend, Ron, in Alaska. To my surprise, he began telling me about the wonderful things God was doing in his life. I could hardly believe my ears because, while Tim had always gone along with his Christian upbringing, there had been no light, no fire, no excitement. Now he was on the phone telling me he had a spring in his step and a sparkle in his eye, and he'd be home in five days to tell me what happened that summer in a church he attended in Anchorage.

That night at dinner, while I was telling the rest of the family about Tim's call, the phone rang. It was the Royal Canadian Mounted Police with the news that Tim and Ron had been killed instantly when a three-ton truck driven by a drunk teenager crossed the center line just outside of Whitehorse and crumpled Tim's little Volkswagen like papier-maché.

I went through the identical emotions that I experienced when my son, Steven, died in Vietnam. I was plunged again into shock and denial. At first I churned with what felt like a knife in my chest. Later, I burned with anger, railing at God for allowing the unthinkable to happen. *Another* son taken . . . *another* deposit in heaven . . . wasn't *one* enough?

Again, tears were a blessed relief for me. I didn't deny Tim's death as much as I had Steven's, but I did burn more vehemently because Tim had died so needlessly, so pointlessly, so carelessly.

We buried Tim on August 12, 1973, five years to the day after we buried Steven. Among the speakers at the memorial service, which was attended by several hundred people, was one of the pastors from the Anchorage church Tim and Ron had attended that summer. He told about the dynamic change in the boys' lives and how they gave public testimony of that change at a baptism he officiated. As I listened, I thought, *How I wish I could have been there to hear Tim share his faith and then see him baptized.*

Two months later, around the middle of October, my husband, Bill, and I journeyed to Whitehorse to pick up some of Tim's personal belongings that were salvaged from his car. We also went to the very spot on the highway where he and Ron were ushered into God's presence. Then we flew to Anchorage to visit the church they attended all summer.

Everyone treated us graciously, and a woman on the church staff gave us a tour of the building that included a tape library with thousands of tapes. She explained that the church makes a tape of every service and when there's not much to do during long Alaskan winters, folks watch the tapes for entertainment. Some folks can't get to church regularly, but when they do come in from the hinterlands, they often take several tapes back home with them. Not only does the church make tapes of all the services, but many folks bring their own recorders to tape the music or the preaching. In Alaska they like to say that folks aren't bookworms; they're *tapeworms!*

After seeing all these tapes, I asked what any mother would: "Do you have the tape of the night Tim was baptized and gave his testimony?" Sadly, she said she was sorry but the service that night had not been taped. She explained that the man who operated the tape-recording equipment was baptized that night, and no one else knew how to push the buttons!

Coming home from Alaska I felt dejected and that God had surely neglected me. Of the thousands of tapes this church recorded, they missed the night Tim gave his testimony. How unfair and cruel could God be?

On December 14, my birthday, a small package came in the mail. It had no return address, but the postmark said Nome, Alaska. I opened the package and found no letter or note, only a well-worn cassette tape that looked as if it had been played a hundred times. Curious, I put the unlabeled cassette into a cassette player, and in a few seconds I heard Tim's excited voice.

"My name is Tim Johnson, and I'm third in the group that came up from California. Funny, we were headed for South America. I don't know how we got here but . . . uh . . . the Lord works in miraculous ways. Praise the Lord! I'm glad He did.

"I was brought up in a Christian home and Christian schools, but after graduation I departed and went my own way. It wasn't until last December that a friend sat down with me and showed me the real way to the Lord—the true way. I was 'on fire' for a couple of months, and then I just fell by the wayside.

"It wasn't until I came to Alaska that things really started happening in my life. Since then, I have a smile on my face, and everyone looks at me like I must have been a sour lemon before. But now it's different, and I'm thankful that I'm here today. Thanks be to God."

The next sound I heard were splashes as Tim was plunged beneath the waters of baptism. As he came up out of the water, I could hear his triumphant words, "Praise the Lord!"

I sat there, stunned. This was the kid who would get embarrassed if we took him to Knott's Berry Farm for his birthday and sang to him. This was the kid whose idea of fun was bringing home funeral bows from the mortuary where he worked and tying them on our pets. This was the kid we had to bribe with a new set of tires to get him to go to Bible conferences.

This was definitely a *miracle*!

How the tape found its way into our home was a miracle too, and it proves God does work in wonderful ways through His people. Later, I learned from the church in Anchorage that one of their members, a bush pilot, heard about my request for a tape of Tim's baptism service. I'm not sure what bush pilots do (I guess they fly around the bushes a lot), but as this pilot made his many trips into the back country, he began asking folks if anyone taped the service the night the boys were baptized.

Finally, he found a fisherman from Nome who visited the church that night and taped the service. Now I know Nome isn't the end of the world, but I am sure you can see the end of the world from there! The bush pilot asked the fisherman to send the tape to me at my home, which he did. It was the best birthday present I could have asked for. It was, indeed, my *miracle tape*.

That tape was played many times during that Christmas season. The tears would roll down my face, but they were tears of joy. In some strange way, listening to Tim's voice helped me accept what had happened. I saw again that God specialized in bringing triumph out of tragedy and joy out of pain. Problems won't disappear because you pretend they don't exist. Your utter helplessness will not magically vanish. Accepting what happens is a vital step to grabbing that rope in the dark that becomes your lifeline.

Adapted from *Mama Get the Hammer! There's a Fly on Papa's Head!* by Barbara Johnson, © Barbara Johnson 1994. Published by Word, Inc., Texas. Used by permission of the author.

Barbara Johnson, (the "Geranium Lady") is a Christian humorist and author of twelve adult books and four books for children. Her books, all bestsellers, have won numerous awards and are reprinted in eleven languages. She founded Spatula Ministries in 1979. Now there are fifty Spatula support groups around the country. Barbara speaks at about twenty-five "Women of Faith"

events each year, which means she has spoken to about 1 million women at these events since 1996. She and her husband, Bill, live in La Habra, California.

The Awakening

Eunice Kauffman

When I learned I was pregnant with our third child, I prayed that this one would be a girl. After having two boys, it seemed a reasonable prayer. The prayer was answered, but later I would have settled for just another healthy child.

Our baby girl seemed perfectly normal at first. We named her Tauni Dawn and she was as beautiful as her name. When she was six months old, I noticed she didn't kick off her covers the way her brothers had at that age. When I expressed concern, my husband ridiculed my fears. But I wouldn't let it go, and insisted that we have our doctor examine her.

The doctor assured us she was "Fine, just fine."

"See, I told you there was nothing to worry about," my husband chided.

But things did not improve, and finally, when Tauni was about a year old, I took her to a specialist in Boise. After X rays and other examinations, the specialist announced that she had cerebral palsy, and bluntly added, "This child has no future."

We were advised to find a permanent place for Tauni to live, but she was too sweet to give up. I couldn't do it. Her shining dark hair and trusting brown eyes, her lovely complexion and her smile tied strings around my heart.

I carried heartache through seemingly endless days and sleepless nights, haunted by questions without answers: *What did I do that might have caused this? What could I have done that might have prevented this from happening?*

By the time Tauni reached her fourth year, her hands were spastic and folded with stiff fingers. She couldn't walk and had to be carried. Her legs did not develop and were too thin to support the dead weight of her body. It was clear I could no longer care for her at home. We took her to reside at a state hospital.

Knowing I had need of God, I turned my thoughts toward Him. I don't believe I could have stood the separation if I had not had the love of the Lord to see me through.

God was right there waiting for me. My Christian friends, Basil and Wilma Lewis, invited me and my children for an overnight stay. They answered my questions about God and Jesus and the Bible. Then they took us to church with them on Sunday morning.

At the end of the service, the pastor gave an altar call. At first I hesitated, but when God nudged me, I got down there fast. I accepted Christ as my Savior and cried so hard I couldn't talk to the counselor. As

I walked back down the aisle, I felt as though I was floating; like my feet weren't touching the floor.

Over time, I drifted from my first love of Jesus and went blundering through life. I didn't let Him be the Lord of my life. My Christian friends had Him in every area of their daily living. I wanted what they had, but didn't understand the importance of reading and studying God's Word and letting go of my own selfish desires.

Then one day I attended a Billy Graham evangelistic meeting. I heard the words, "Jesus is God, and until you believe He is God, your spiritual growth will be hindered."

It was the first time I had ever paid attention to those words. It was an awakening for me. I began attending weekly Bible study classes, went to Christian seminars, read wonderful Christian books and associated with committed Christian friends. I grew in love for the Lord. God put me back together again.

As I look back, though, I realize it was my daughter who first turned me to Christ. If she had been a normal child, I question whether I would have felt the need for His love. She couldn't talk. She didn't recognize me as her mother. She didn't know if it was summer or winter, Christmas or Fourth of July. Sadly, she did not progress at all through the twenty-six years she lived on this earth. But I learned much from her, and through her, about utter dependence on God and His grace.

Do not be anxious about anything, but in
everything, by prayer and petition, with

thanksgiving, present your requests to God.
And the peace of God, which transcends
all understanding, will guard your hearts
and your minds in Christ Jesus.
(Philippians 4:6-7)

Eunice (Nelson) Kauffman, author of *Résumé of the Bible*, now lives in Payette, Idaho. While living in Boise, she led Bible studies at the state prison and county jail and was a counselor for Reachout Hotline with Prison Fellowship. She attended Billy Graham's School of Christian Writing in Minneapolis, Minnesota. Eunice writes gospel poetry and is an award-winning artist with watercolors, acrylics and pastels. She is a member of Christian Writers of Idaho.

Shape Up or Move Out!

Diane Maxey

After twenty years of marriage, my husband left me for a young woman barely three years older than our oldest daughter. Our two teenagers took it hard. Although our daughter was the first to fall apart and certainly went through her share of despairing moments, it was my quiet son who took the hardest and longest turn downward.

Even though both children knew God and had been raised in Sunday school, they felt that God wasn't there for them and that somehow He should and could have prevented the events that tore our family apart. When He didn't, they were mad at Him. What a difficult time, dealing with my own raw emotions as well as those of my children.

My first clue that my son, Kenny, was headed for trouble came when I got a call from a local police department that he had been caught trying to fish money out of a parking meter at the beach. When they searched him, they found a small amount of marijuana.

Although I was angry with him, I somehow brushed off the drugs. My son was good at making excuses, and I was eager to believe them.

At the same time, he rebelled against going to church with me. I coerced him into going to church through junior high, but he grew more and more sullen into his high school years. He refused to respond or participate, no matter how much of an interest his youth leader took in him. I finally gave in and told him that I could not make him want to go to church and that the next time he attended, it would be because he wanted to, not because I was making him go. Although I had prayed about it and sought counsel from the youth director, it was one of those decisions that left me wondering if I was doing the right thing.

My son continued his downward spiral. He flunked most of his classes and started hanging out with the wrong crowd. For a long time I continued to believe that he was the "good guy" and that it was the rest of them who were "bad." Eventually I had to admit that my son was as involved in drugs, alcohol and lawlessness as any of the others. He eventually got kicked out of regular school, then dropped out of continuation school. He worked a part-time job but mostly hung out with his friends. Occasionally he would stumble home to eat, sleep and clean up. Then he would be off again.

One day as I was driving home from church, the Old Testament story of Eli, the priest, came to mind. I recalled how God had sternly warned him that his sons were evil and that it was Eli's responsibility to do something about it. God warned Eli that if he did not do something about it, it would be on his head. Suddenly, I was filled with the fearful realization that I had allowed my son to live in my home when I knew full well that he was engaged in drugs and all other kinds of evil. It was a wake-up call that it was time to take action.

I prayed fervently, and that night I gave him the choice—either clean up his act, in which case he was welcome to continue living at home, or move out. He professed the desire to live right, but quickly showed that it was just talk. I demanded that he move out. It was Thanksgiving weekend, no less, and was without a doubt one of the most difficult things I had ever done. He moved about slowly as he gathered a few things, all the while hoping I'd give him a last-minute reprieve. Oh how I wanted to, but my fear of the Lord and His Word to me helped me to stand my ground.

Kenny worked a part-time job and had nowhere to go but to bounce from friend to friend. Now what would happen to him? I had to leave him in God's hands.

Three months later, he called me in desperation. The drugs he had abused had left him utterly paranoid. He saw evil spirits all around him and confessed to me that he thought himself unredeemable because he knew God and yet had rejected Him. That night I got out my Bible and read him verse after verse about God's redeeming and saving power. He asked me over and over again to show him in black-and-white where it said these things.

After a three-day struggle, we wound up with a local pastor of a friend of mine. He recommended a drug and alcohol ministry called U-Turn for Christ. Kenny had tried one drug rehab but left within three days, so I had dim hopes that he would go. Our meeting with the pastor that day seemed absurd. Kenny was so ravaged by the drugs that he could barely sit up straight and kept falling asleep as we talked. The pastor was patient, and my son eventually agreed to give U-Turn a try.

On the drive out, I began sharing with him some of my personal experiences with God. I found myself sharing the time when I had come to the realization as an adult that I did not trust God, and that all I could do was plead with Him to help me because I didn't know how. Suddenly my son was convulsing in tears, literally sobbing in remorse for his life and pleading for the Lord to save him. I pulled to the side of the road, where we sat and prayed for over an hour.

I would like to say that from that point on it was a breeze, but that isn't real life. His entire countenance changed, and even the older men at the ranch would share with me how they marveled at his knowledge of the Word for such a young man. But three times my son left the U-Turn ministry to taste the world again, only to return shortly thereafter. There was no doubt that God was moving mightily in his life.

Then another miracle occurred. Under completely separate circumstances, his father, who by then had been divorced from his second wife, asked Jesus into his life and was born again. A couple of years later, after some real soul-searching and getting reacquainted, we reconciled in marriage.

In the meantime, Kenny stabilized in his walk and eventually became an overseer in the U-Turn for Christ ministry. He was invited on a short-term mission trip to the Philippines to visit a Filipino pastor. During this visit, he was introduced to one of the pastor's daughters, Fely Gantalao. He came home smitten, although he was reluctant to admit it because he felt it diminished his original purpose in going on the trip, which was to spread the gospel.

A few months later he was back in the Philippines at the direction of his own pastor, helping U-Turn for Christ establish an orphanage. It was during this time that he courted Fely and asked her to marry him.

Barely one year later our entire family traveled to the Philippines to witness our son take the hand of his beautiful bride in marriage. God had taken him halfway around the world to meet a beautiful, godly young Christian woman. As if that weren't enough, later that same year he was ordained as a pastor. He and his wife now serve together as director and house parents for ten children at the orphanage.

As we left the Philippines, my son hugged me and thanked me for my years of love and prayers. He then got a smile on his face and said he thanked me most for kicking him out.

How ironic! The most difficult thing I had to do was the very thing that produced the repentance that was required to turn him back to God.

 Diane Maxey is Vice President of Administration for a large insurance company. She has been involved in women's ministries for over thirty years as a teacher, mentor, writer, editor and speaker. She and her husband, Ken, lead worship at Calvary Chapel Grass Mountain Fellowship in Green Valley, California, north of Los Angeles.

E-mail: dianemaxey@hotmail.com

A Daughter's Decision

Stanley Tam

When our youngest daughter, Candy, was a sophomore in college, she wrote to Juanita and me, "January 21 is your wedding anniversary. I've decided to come home and take you out to dinner. I'm free after lunch on Friday. I can drive back Sunday afternoon and be ready for my first class Monday."

"She shouldn't do that!" I said to Juanita. "Call and tell her we appreciate her thoughtfulness, but—"

My wife nudged me, held up the letter and said, "Read all of it, Stanley." The letter continued, "We'll make it a double celebration, because I have something wonderful to tell you!"

"Uh, oh," I commented.

"Sounds serious," Juanita said. Her eyes sparkled as only a mother's eyes can on such occasions. Then she grew serious and added, "We've got to help her think sensibly. She has two more years of college."

Candy pulled into our driveway at 5 o'clock.

145

"Ready to go?" she sang out, entering the house. "I thought we'd eat at that restaurant I like so much over in Ada. Would you please drive, Daddy? Then I can tell you about my big surprise. If I wait to tell you after we get to the restaurant, I'll be too excited to eat."

As we headed east out of Lima, we expected Candy to begin talking. Instead, she sat mute in the back seat. I glanced at my wife. She looked at me with raised eyebrows. But neither of us spoke.

Finally, when we were almost to Maysville, our daughter began. "You're waiting to hear what I have to say," she half-whispered.

"We won't hear anything," her mother said gently, "unless you talk a little bit louder."

Silence again.

"We want to hear," Juanita prompted.

We passed through Maysville and came to the junction, where we turned to head north. A billboard advertised the restaurant as three miles farther, just at the outskirts of Ada.

"Mom, Dad," Candy began, measuring each word, "I've fallen in love."

"What?" my wife and I exclaimed in unison. Then Juanita quickly added, "That's wonderful!"

"It's about time, isn't it?" I said.

"Tells us about him," Juanita added.

My wife and I were now the excited ones, chattering like a couple of children. There was no traffic, so I slowed the car to a crawl.

"What's his name?" Juanita asked.

She gave us his name, and then blurted out, "He's asked me to marry him, and I told him yes."

"Is he a college student like you?" I inquired.

"N-no."

"He's a Christian?" Juanita asked.

"Oh, sure, Mom! You know me better than to ask that!"

We reached the restaurant and I pulled into a parking spot. But we all remained in the car.

"If he's not in college," my wife probed, "how old is he?"

"Thirty something. . . ."

"Candy!" I spoke so loudly Juanita touched my knee. "Isn't that quite a spread in age?"

"You're not out of your teens," Juanita said quietly.

"But when you meet him, you'll understand," our daughter countered. "I go out with guys my age on campus, and they're such nerds. But he's different. He knows how to treat a girl on a date. He makes me feel like a queen."

We sounded her out further, learning that this chap was a divorced man with a house full of children.

"It's one thing to adjust to marriage," Juanita counseled. "But to come home from the honeymoon to a house full of children. . . ."

"I'll be honored to raise his children for him," Candy insisted. "Wait until you meet him. Wait until you see how wonderful he is."

"It doesn't seem to me your mother and I have any business meeting this man," I said. Afterward, I was sorry for having spoken so bluntly. Silence now permeated that car like a steel band at the plant drawn tight to secure one of our plastics shipments.

In full honesty, I can affirm that I was concerned about our darling daughter. But I was concerned about Stanley Tam as well. What would people think? Our neighbors? At the plant? At church? When I stood up to speak at meetings?

"I should have known," I heard Candy mutter in disgust.

"Shall we go into the restaurant?" Juanita asked.

"I'm not hungry!" our daughter huffed.

We drove home in utter silence. I had hardly stopped the car when Candy burst out and ran to the door. She had her own key and hurried inside to her room where she locked the door.

She didn't come down all the next day. Juanita tried to interest her in food but she only muttered incoherently.

Saturday night came and passed. Sunday morning, too. We always looked forward to having Candy attend worship with us when she returned for visits. But not this day.

Afternoon came and soon it would be time for a very disappointed and disgruntled young lady to drive back to college.

"Stanley!" Juanita prodded. "You can't just sit there doing nothing!"

So I trudged up the stairs and knocked on the locked door.

"Umf!" Candy responded.

"Your mother and I want to have open minds," I said painfully. "Come down and let's talk about the situation."

Our daughter, bright-eyed, joined us in the living room. She had obviously read too much into my statement of wanting to be open minded.

I stammered for a few moments, never getting to the point. Candy began glancing at the clock. So I suggested that, as we always did when she left us, we go to our knees for a parting prayer. All three of us participated, although I can't remember one word that was uttered.

After our prayer, Juanita helped Candy get her things together. I pressed some money into our daughter's hand and gave her a dutiful kiss on the cheek. I thought I saw tears in her eyes as she headed straight to the door and outside, not looking back.

My wife and I stood at the window, watching. When her car was out of sight, I grasped Juanita by the shoulders and moved her back to where we had just knelt. Together, we poured out our hearts to the Lord, imploring Him to look after our baby daughter, asking His forgiveness for failures on our own part.

One month went by. Two months. Three.

My Thursday-noon prayer partner had recently gone through a similar circumstance. Now it was my turn. Every Thursday, Art and I met for prayer. Every morning and every night, Juanita and I prayed together. Again and again at work, I would stop what I was doing, bow at my desk and ask the Lord to help our dear Candy.

"I ask for You not to let her miss Your will, Lord," I prayed.

That prayer really convicted me because I had to admit that, so long as our daughter obeyed the Lord, whatever happened would have His blessing.

I felt a new tenderness come to my heart. I regretted the harsh words I had spoken to Candy. As a result, I became much more tolerant toward our staff. Weekends, when on speaking engagements, I sensed a difference, a warmth and an abundant unction. Yet I held back.

One night Juanita said in tears, "I took this matter to the Lord today. I asked Him to carry out His will and to give me the courage to accept whatever that may be!"

Thank God for Christian women like my Juanita!

Candy wrote as before, telling us about classes, her friends in the dorm and activities at the church she attended. She didn't mention her boyfriend. We tried to be loving and positive in our letters to her, giving hints of our willingness to stand by her decision.

Then, at last, she wrote us with the real news: "Mom and Dad, I love you so much! You can never know how much. I wouldn't do anything to hurt you. But I also know you don't want me to hinder myself just to please you. I've been praying much about the future, about how things could be twenty years from now. Thank you for all the lessons you've taught me about seeking God's will for our lives. Well, that's what I've been doing. And I know I've done what the Lord wants me to do, not just what would please you. I have broken up with Gary."

What a mighty answered prayer! What maturity in our daughter!

And what a change in me—my ministry has never been the same since!

From *God's Woodshed: The Power of a Cleansed Life*, by Stanley Tam, ©1991 by Horizon Books.

Dr. Stanley Tam is President of United States Plastics Corporation and States Smelting and Refining of Lima, Ohio. Starting with $37, he built his business into a multi-million-dollar enterprise serving most of the giant corporations in America today. But as he points out repeatedly in *God's Woodshed*, from which the above chapter is taken, the credit is not his: His success came after he literally and legally turned his entire business over to God. He points out in the book, "There are no VIPs on God's roster of servants."

Dr. Tam is author of three books, including *God Owns My Business* (also published by Horizon Books), with over 400,000 copies in print in eight languages. Two films have been made about Dr. Tam's life: "God Is My Senior Partner" and "The Answer."

The Year I Didn't Cry Much

Glenda Palmer

I didn't cry much that year—and I'm a crier. I cry at happy weddings and sad movies. I even cry when we sing "How Great Thou Art" in church. But the "impossible year" when our twenty-two-year-old son had cancer, I didn't cry much.

It started with Kent complaining, "My back hurts so bad, I can hardly surf."

I made him a doctor's appointment, but wasn't especially concerned. Kent worked in construction and was active in sports. He had probably "tweaked" his back on that recent ski trip.

But after all the tests the surgeon called and said he wanted to admit Kent immediately. "It looks like a large tumor. It may be malignant."

When I hung up the phone, I cried a little and I begged God, "Please don't take my baby away."

After his surgery, I didn't cry much when the doctor said words like "disappointed," "chemotherapy" and "nine-pound tumor."

During the next months, Kent, his brother Scott, my husband and I did what we had to do. And we laughed a lot. This surprised me. I had thought if I ever faced the possibility of losing a child, I would weep continuously. But I didn't cry much.

Each morning, I studied my Bible. Those words were my marching orders for the day. Hymns and praise songs were God speaking to me and me to Him. The Lord sent specific people to minister to me and pray without ceasing for Kent. God's grace! Yes! It was sufficient! It really was, whatever the outcome.

Kent checked into the hospital five times for chemotherapy, one week in and one week out. He lost all his hair and got sicker and sicker. On the way to the hospital for the last treatment he said, "I'd rather die than go through this again."

But he checked in. That day I cried, but I didn't cry much.

Between hospital stays, Kent took classes to become a real estate agent. I admired his positive attitude.

When the chemotherapy was over, two small tumors remained on his aorta, the main heart artery. Kent's doctor suggested a surgeon in Indianapolis who specialized in that kind of intricate cancer surgery. I prayed and fasted, but I didn't cry much.

On Thanksgiving Day, six weeks before our trip to Indianapolis, my mother died after an extended illness. Daddy asked me to read the 23rd Psalm to her as she passed away. "Yea, though I walk through the valley of the shadow of death, I will fear no evil: for thou art with me" (Psalm 23:4, KJV). I knew that feeling. Mother was my best friend but I didn't cry much.

When the Indianapolis surgeon said, "I removed the tumors. They aren't malignant," I hugged him and wept, but not long. I had a lot of people to call and tell about our great and mighty God whose grace is sufficient.

Now, ten years later, Kent is alive and well, happily married and works as a mortgage lender. Once again, I cry at weddings, movies and, most of all, when I sing "How Great Thou Art."

Glenda Palmer has authored sixteen children's picture books as well as a variety of stories, articles, greeting cards and songs. Currently, Glenda is an instructor with the Institute of Children's Literature. She and her husband Richard live near their two married sons in San Diego County, California, and attend Shadow Mountain Community Church.

E-mail: glenda@juno.com

With Wings As Eagles

Diana L. James

I glanced up at the clock above my son's hospital bed. I thought sadly of the painful hours and the many hospital beds Rick had occupied over the past six months. I thought how his life and the lives of our entire family had changed since the day he was struck and thrown from his motorcycle by a speeding car. On the bedside table was a Little League team picture and close-up photo of Rick's eleven-year-old son, Ricky. Rick and Ricky had laughed and played horseshoes together at a family picnic only the day before the accident, but neither of them were laughing anymore.

There was a serious problem with Rick's left leg. The injuries to his shoulder and face had healed, leaving only a few scars. But a deep area of missing flesh just above his ankle would not heal.

Twice the doctors had attempted the difficult ten-hour "muscle flap" operation, by which a muscle from the patient's stomach, shoulder or back is grafted over the open wound. Twice the procedure had failed,

leaving Rick physically exhausted and emotionally de-
spondent. The doctors were considering amputation if
the third muscle flap operation did not work.

"I can't take another operation. I know I'll die on
the operating table if they try that operation again,"
Rick told me over and over again.

My reassuring words did nothing to soothe Rick's
fears, and I noticed that even my own positive attitude was beginning to waver. Although I'd been
praying for Rick's healing since the day of the accident, I began to feel my prayers were inadequate. I
called the prayer group from my church and two
other prayer lines to ask for help.

In addition to physical healing, I knew Rick
needed a healing of his spirit. Witnesses to the accident had told him it was a miracle he hadn't been
killed. During the early part of his recuperation, Rick
said he was sure God must have had a reason for
sparing his life. But when the two operations on his
leg failed, and as the days in the hospital turned into
weeks and months, he started believing that perhaps
he was meant to die after all.

It seemed that nothing could lift Rick out of his
mood of hopelessness and despair. Attempting to
cheer him up, his three brothers told jokes and read
him the comics. I even tried singing to him, but nothing worked.

Then one day I brought in my Bible and began to
read aloud. At first he paid no attention. The next
day I tried again. This time I read Isaiah 40:31, "They
that wait upon the LORD shall renew their strength;
they shall mount up with wings as eagles; they shall

run, and not be weary; and they shall walk, and not faint" (KJV). For the first time in a long time I saw a flicker of interest on Rick's face.

I immediately thought of the ceramic eagle I had on my desk at home with that same Scripture verse engraved on a plaque on the pedestal base, beneath the outstretched wings. The next day I brought my eagle to the hospital and placed it close to Rick's bed.

When I came back to see Rick that evening he seemed to be in a better mood than he had been in a long time. Little by little over the next few days I saw his spirits brighten. I asked his nurses about it and they told me that almost every time any of them entered Rick's room he was reading aloud the verse on the bottom of the eagle statue.

A few days later, Rick unexpectedly informed the doctors he was ready to have the third (and last possible) muscle flap operation on his leg. This time they would use the large muscle from Rick's back. They could not use just a portion of the muscle, but had to use it all, wrapping it around his leg. If the operation was successful, there would be a "debulking" operation several months later to remove the excess muscle after the missing flesh on his leg filled in. If the operation was not successful—well, I couldn't bear to think about that.

There was something different about Rick the day they wheeled him into the operating room. Because this was an unusual operation, there were several extra doctors and medical students there to observe the procedure. Rick greeted them all with cheery confidence. Just before they put the anesthesia mask over his face, he grinned and assured the group, "Don't worry. Everything's going to be fine. God's in charge."

Rick was right, God was in charge and everything went just fine. This time the operation worked. This time his leg did not reject the muscle. Oh, there was terrible pain in his back and leg and sometimes there still is, but Rick has a good life, two legs and an unshakable belief in the power of prayer. He now collects statues and posters of eagles to remind him of his favorite Bible verse.

Diana L. James is the editor/compiler of *Bounce Back*, *Bounce Back Too*, *Teens Can Bounce Back* and this book, all four published by Horizon Books. Her stories and articles have also appeared in numerous magazines and fifteen book compilations. She speaks for churches, writers' conferences and Christian women's groups. Diana is founder and past President of Christian Writers of Idaho, and is radio host of "Encouraging Words," an inspirational radio interview program heard daily throughout southwestern Idaho and eastern Oregon on KBXL-FM 94.1, Boise.

Website: www.dianajames.com
E-mail: dianajames@aol.com

Section 5

Parents

Honor your father and your mother,
so that you may live long in the land the
LORD your God is giving you.
(Exodus 20:12)

Miracle in the Rain

Jan Coleman

As my daughter Jennifer raced up a mountain freeway one dismal winter morning two years ago, even the fierce El Niño rainstorm didn't slow her down. But when her sport utility vehicle hydroplaned, it flipped upside down, along with my world as I knew it.

My husband, Carl, and I inched our way to the hospital, driving through the streams that gushed over the roadway. We had no details of the accident, only that Jennifer had been airlifted to the trauma center twenty miles away. I was paralyzed with fear that her recklessness had finally brought disaster, and my heart cried out, *Please, Lord, don't let my daughter die with a wall still between us!*

For the past year, Jen had been on a mad dash from her problems. With her marriage falling apart, her natural spunk had given way to sparring gloves; every family gathering somehow turned into a jabbing match. Outwardly she seemed shockproof, in complete control; but inside my daughter was still a fragile young girl aching for the father who had abandoned our family years before. She was still punishing the rest of us for her broken childhood dreams. I had frantically tried to mend each rip in her life with a mother's counsel and correction (and tips on how to patch the marriage) but my unwelcome words only made her more angry and defensive. I was at my wit's end; she hadn't spoken to me in over two months.

At the trauma center, the neurosurgeon grimly told us, "She has a serious head injury and is in very bad shape."

I thought, *This is where the rubber meets the road when it comes to my faith, isn't it?*

Down in the hospital chapel we found Jen's husband, Steve.

"We had a terrible fight last night, and I said some awful things," he said. That seemed to give more perspective on the accident.

As I prayed for my daughter, I thought of the verse, "All things work together for good to them that love God" (Romans 8:28, KJV). *All things?* I inwardly dissented. *Even tragic car accidents?*

Then it hit me. Fretting would not change the outcome. If I trusted God, I had no choice but to cast all doubts aside. My daughter's life was in His hands.

Jen lay in a coma, her swollen, shaved head hooked to tubes, wires and pressure monitors. Machines blipped and beeped while nurses worked frantically to keep her blood pressure stable; death could steal her at any moment. If she did survive, brain damage was likely. We just didn't know to what degree.

I prayed, *Lord give me your perspective on this. My eyes are too blurry.* At that moment, she appeared so peaceful, so beautiful; and I knew God was doing His restoration work while she slept.

Suddenly, a strange voice rang out behind me: "How's my girl?" I turned to see a young hospital technician. "Oh, hello. I'm Phillip. I was at the accident scene with this little lady."

Then Phillip told us his story. He'd been heading down the mountain when he saw a massive billow of water ahead, and a tiny dot catapult from it. He knew it must be a body. Jen had been thrown from the car as it tumbled. She landed on the freeway just inches from where the mangled vehicle had come to rest.

"I was very late to work, but something told me I had to stop," Phillip explained.

The highway patrol officer who was first on the scene had found no breathing, no pulse; and he had covered Jen's curled, lifeless body with a yellow slicker. He was calling the coroner when Phillip pulled up.

"She's not going to make it," the officer said.

"I won't believe that!" Phillip shot back. He was an orthopedic technician, trained as a navy field medic. He quickly went to work on her.

After a few minutes, she gasped a breath, just as another car pulled up—it was an off-duty emergency medical technician with a respirator in his car!

As Phillip told us this, I could see Jesus darting over to Jen, reaching out His arms to catch her, His body cushioning her against a deadly fall, one that could have broken her entire body. And God had cleared the raging skies so a rescue helicopter could finally land.

It was then that I understood what it means to feel the peace that passes all understanding. Jennifer's condition was not a hopeful one according to the doctor's charts, but it didn't matter. God had His own charts.

The next day Carl and I went to church, and when I opened the bulletin I shook my head in disbelief at the sermon title: "God's Purpose for My Problems." It was about how our response to problems reveals what we believe about God: Are we shaken by circumstances that seem bleak and hopeless, or are we grounded in simple trust that He knows best?

Later, when I shared this with Steve, he put his arm around me and said, "Whatever happens, I know God has allowed it, and even if she is disabled, I'm committed to this marriage forever."

Already changes were occurring in all of us. We knew Jennifer was safe in God's hands.

Five days later, Jen began to twitch her feet and emerge from the coma. She was not paralyzed! Excitement brewed within me—what miracle would God do next?

I should have known. My former husband, whom we hadn't seen for ten years, showed up at the hospital.

"She's just like I was," he said, "reckless and immature, running away from herself. If I hadn't walked out on you, none of this would have happened. I'm sorry I messed up our marriage, Jan."

How long I had waited to hear those words!

"I forgave you long ago," I told him as he broke down in tears. We wept together, and I felt God's grace pour over me as I saw how tormented Bob was, in bondage to his guilt. Any remnants of anger between us flowed away.

Ten days later Jen was transferred to a rehab hospital. "We've never seen such progress," the doctor said. Her fighting spirit kicked in over the weeks as she struggled to walk again, to formulate sentences, even to chew her food. She *needed* her strong will now.

Three months after the accident, we helped Jennifer walk shakily into her own house, back to Steve and their two little boys. "I'm so grateful that God is a God of second chances," she said, misty-eyed.

It's been two years since the accident now, and her bruised brain continues to heal. She's still feisty, but now I discern a refreshing softness that I've not seen before.

"Mom," she told me one day, "I never want to be estranged from you again. I realize now how much you love me and want the best for me."

People in our small town still talk about the miracle in the rain, how incredible it was for a young woman to be thrown from her car, hurled 100 feet, land on her head and survive—not just that, but to be almost as good as she was before.

But the real miracle to me, the *best* miracle, is to have my daughter back.

Jan Coleman is a speaker and full-time writer whose articles appear regularly in national magazines and story collections. She specializes in personal experience stories. Jan lives in the northern California gold rush country where she loves junking for treasures and antiques.

She and her husband love to travel,
and she is working on her first book.

E-mail: jwriter@foothill.net

The Sweet Road of Reconciliation

Jim Clark

For several years Patti Davis poured much of her energy into venting anger toward her parents. She was estranged from them for years. Yet when she received news of her father's serious illness, the venom suddenly ceased to flow. As a result, she is now feasting on the riches of a mended relationship.

You may not recognize the name Patti Davis until you hear of her famous parents—Ronald and Nancy Reagan. Patti is the daughter from Ronald's second marriage. For many of her forty-three years, Patti lived in rebellion to Mom and Dad. She dated men completely opposite from her father. While Dad was in the White House, Patti was hanging out with men sporting ponytails and riding Harley Davidson motorcycles.

Patti briefly followed her aspirations in acting. Another talent began to blossom, however, when she lingered over a computer, tapping away her thoughts. Sadly, Patti's early writing career oozed with bitterness. She wrote three books blasting her family, un-covering their various dysfunctions.

Patti described her mother as manipulative, her father as cold and remote. Patti's bitter memoirs raised a dividing wall between her and the Reagans. When she moved to New York City, her only contact was to leave a forwarding address. Yet the warmth of one man's persistence began to thaw her cold war. That man was her dad.

Ronald had often attempted to stay in touch, yet in his retirement his messages became more urgent. Life was slipping away. He felt the need to reach out and be close to his little girl.

Patti gradually faced her own cruelty. She realized she had been as brutal to her mother as Nancy had been to her. Then came the devastating news about her dad.

The onset of Ronald Reagan's Alzheimer's disease set in motion a beautiful healing process in this wounded family. Two weeks after hearing of her dad's diagnosis, Patti called the family and apolo-gized for the pain she inflicted. The cold war was coming to a close. She was ready to write a new story of her family, a story of family peace.

As Patti opened the door of forgiveness to her par-ents, other mangled relationships began to heal. She's now growing closer to her siblings. On a recent Father's Day, an unusual mood of harmony perme-ated the Reagan home as the children gathered in Los Angeles. One of the sons, Michael, is now relish-ing the hugs from his father he yearned for during his earlier years. Grandchildren enjoy races with

Grandpa in the pool. A mood of peace has settled upon this once-warring family—a peace many of us long to enjoy in our family relationships.

In her book, *The Healing Presence* [Grand Rapids, MI: Baker Books, 1995], Leanne Payne suggests that three hurdles stand in the way for a Christian to discover true wholeness in Christ. One is the lack of self-acceptance. The other two have to do with forgiveness—failing to receive forgiveness from God and a failure to forgive others. In order for people to gain wholeness in their lives, they must honestly deal with the separations in their lives.

All of us have experienced a fallout with family and friends. Have you noticed you harbor some of your strongest feelings of bitterness toward those who are supposed to love you? Dad's role is to protect us. Mom is expected to cherish us. Christian friends are meant to reflect Christ's love. When we're let down by those closest to our hearts, we often hit a rocky bottom.

How will you mend your broken relationships? Jesus gives you the first step: "If your brother sins against you, go and show him his fault, just between the two of you" (Matthew 18:15). Whatever conflict you may now have with a significant person in your life, decide today to build a bridge back to that heart. Seek God's forgiveness. Ask Him to give you strength and courage to take that difficult first step. Then watch the Lord of reconciliation do His healing work.

And remember this crucial truth of human relationships—even if the person who hurt you never accepts your offer of reconciliation, you can keep your heart uncluttered from the refuse of bitterness. Do all you can to forgive and be forgiven. Then entrust this estranged relationship to the Father and go on with your life as a free person.

You may be protesting: "But Jim, you have no idea how deeply this person hurt me. How could I *possibly* forgive him? And why do I have to forgive? He's in the wrong. It's not fair!"

I've felt the same way. You're right. Forgiveness doesn't seem fair.

Reflect on this thought—where there is forgiveness and reconciliation, there's always a price someone must pay. Always. And when you offer the olive branch to a person who has brought you harm, you risk the possibility of its not being accepted. Forgiveness is risky—a risk the Heavenly Father took in sending His one and only Son to die for us. Not everyone will accept this offer of love.

As I wrote this chapter, I noticed on my bookshelf a crown of thorns. Lying across it is a large metal spike. I walked over to the thorns and, for a moment, ruminated over this symbol of suffering. Then I cradled it gently in my hands and slowly began to squeeze it. As I felt the sharp thorns pricking my hands, I caught just a tiny glimpse of what my Savior endured so I could be forgiven. Reconciled. Free.

Christ did nothing to deserve His death. I was the one in the wrong, the one who deserved His sufferings. But He took my place on the cross.

Yes, forgiveness *is* costly. Someone must always pay the price. Yet how sweet the fellowship that flows between those whose hearts are knit together by the threads of forgiveness.

Patti Davis has enjoyed such sweetness in her dad's sunset years. She now tells of her reluctance to date men who are not enough like her father. The telecast of Richard Nixon's funeral brought her to tears. Not for Nixon, but in anticipation of her own dad's state funeral. She now knows how much she'll miss him. Even in the pain, Patti is enjoying her walk on the sweet road of reconciliation.

I hope you can do the same. Begin that walk by following in the steps of the One who walked down that path to Calvary—to pave your way to the Father. Then welcome others on that road as you pass on forgiveness to them. Family, friends, even enemies.

Jesus is extending His nail-pierced hand to guide you down that road. Won't you join Him?

From *Daily Courage* by Jim Clark, © 1999 by Horizon Books.

Jim Clark has had a varied career in film and video production, script writing, church leadership and pastoral counseling. He is Response Minister for Herald of Truth media ministries. Jim has a Bachelor of Arts degree in Business-economics, an M.A.R. from Harding Graduate School of Religion and an M.Div. from Abilene Christian University. He is author of the book *Daily Courage* (Horizon Books, 1999).

E-mail: jimclark@abilene.com

Our Best Gift for Mother

Susan Titus Osborn

When my mother woke up that August morning in 1993, she felt fine and had a busy day planned. She never dreamed that at 11:15 a.m. her life would change drastically. Her schedule of luncheons, bridge foursomes, painting lessons and beauty salon appointments would be canceled—forever.

I learned about it when I came home and turned on the telephone answering machine. My sister's words rang in my head as I played them over again, hoping I had misunderstood the message: "Mother has had a massive stroke. She can't speak and she's paralyzed on her right side. The doctors don't know if she will survive."

I caught a plane to Arizona and prayed all the way. By the time I drove into the hospital parking lot, my heart was pounding. The walk down the corridor to my mother's room was one of the longest I have taken in my life. I paused for a quick prayer at the door before entering her room.

It was hard to see her lying in that hospital bed, being fed intravenously through a tube—unable to focus her eyes, unable to sit up or even to hold her head up. I tried to comfort her, but didn't know if she was even aware of my presence.

By the following week, my mother had made a remarkable improvement and was expected to live. I walked to her bedside, bent down and took her hand. She reached over with her fingers and felt my right ring finger to see if I was wearing the garnet ring she had given me for my birthday several years before. I was, and she smiled when she recognized it—and thus me. To this day I make sure I wear it on every visit.

My husband, Dick, and I traveled back and forth from Southern California to Phoenix often during those first few months of her recovery. Through physical therapy and caring nurses, her progress continued to be amazing. At that point my husband Dick and I committed to visit Mother every other month for as long as she was alive.

I prayed that she would be able to live a quality life and that God would give me the wisdom to know how to pray specifically for her. For years Mother had experienced many ghosts in the closets of her mind. I could find no way to help her set them free. They imprisoned her. On that day I prayed that God would heal her troubled heart, as well as her incapacitated body. I wanted her to find peace.

I thought of that prayer almost a year later when I once again visited Mother. She still couldn't walk or carry on a conversation. However, she *was* eating on her own, and she could maneuver her electric wheelchair with her left hand. The nurses laughingly claimed she was a road hazard in the halls of the nursing facility. Sometimes they had to turn the motor of the wheelchair off to keep her from bumping into other residents.

Part of Mother's therapy included art, one of her favorite hobbies before the stroke. She started painting with her left hand at the age of seventy-six. Her therapist framed several of her projects, and we had the honor of going to the facility where her art therapy classes were held to see her creations hanging in the halls. Several of them were quite good—bowls of fruit, scenes and portraits. One of the drawings showed a huge shadow across the painting, which represented her limited vision due to the massive stroke. It gave us a small insight into her visual world.

Today at eighty-one she hasn't regained her ability to speak in spite of much therapy, but she can say a few words. Occasionally she says an entire sentence or writes one down, but her vocabulary is limited. She communicates best with her facial expressions. These make known her thoughts about what is being said or done. We've learned to keep our conversations short and light-hearted.

Dick and I have also learned how to transport Mother, so we're able to take her out to lunch when we're in Phoenix. We continue to frequent the Chinese, Mexican and seafood restaurants that were her favorites before the stroke. If the weather permits, we take her sightseeing in the park, to museums and to art galleries. She loves being pushed around in her wheelchair in the fresh air. She enjoys going for an outing, but tires easily and is always ready to go back to the nursing facility she now calls home.

As we push her through the halls of her new home, we are constantly stopping so she can greet the other residents with a smile or a squeeze of her left hand. Several of the staff have admitted she is one of their favorite residents.

Her world has shrunk, but she is content. Once she was a wealthy woman with many worldly possessions. Now she has few that she is able to enjoy, but material things don't matter to her anymore.

All the ghosts in the closets of her mind have escaped. They no longer haunt her. Her priorities have changed. Relationships are now more important to her than material possessions. She truly seems at peace—an answer to my prayers.

When we visit her, we usually take a gift. On several occasions we took her a bouquet of flowers. Several times we took her Beanie Baby cats. She seemed to enjoy putting them in her lap and stroking them, but one can only buy so many cats. Recently, we've been looking for new ideas. I asked Mother, "What can I bring you?"

She smiled and pointed to Dick and me. The gift she wanted was our presence, our companionship. That was what mattered most to her.

In this fast-paced world we live in, most people's schedules are incredibly busy. But if our loved ones are to recover from physical or mental challenges, they need a cheering section. For that reason we—Dick and I, our children and my sister and her family—try to spend as much time with Mother as we can, loving and encouraging her. The greatest gift we can offer her is ourselves.

Susan Titus Osborn is director of the Christian Communicator Manuscript Critique Service and a contributing editor of *The Christian Communicator* magazine. She has authored twenty-four books and numerous articles, devotionals and curriculum materials. Susan is a publisher's representative for Broadman & Holman Publishers and Concordia Publishing House. She is also an adjunct professor at Hope International University in Fullerton, California.

E-mail: Susanosb@aol.com.

A Father's Commitment

Michael E. Phillips

lood was pouring from his nose, and inwardly I laughed. It was easy to find humor in the situation when the blood wasn't mine. My fourteen-year-old opponent cursed profusely under his helmet as I walked away with an airy jaunt—knowing that my key block had both dislodged his helmet and sent our halfback on a fifty-yard scoring run. Then I quickly changed my shoe to kick the extra point.

The score was now 64-0! Today, our team had been virtually invincible. My phlegmatic coach was hopping around on the sidelines like a Rose Bowl winner. Of course, this was only a peewee league in Canada, but he, along with the rest of us, was relishing this victory with pride and confidence—we were the best!

In particular, I had ample reason to feel good: I had successfully kicked all nine extra points. And playing left guard, I was one key in our running attack, which that day picked up over 650 yards. We never swerved from our running style, throwing only one pass the entire game. I was also sent in on defense in short yardage situations to beef up the line. But even with these accomplishments, I felt disappointed.

I hadn't seen my dad at the game, and he'd promised to watch me play. I had never performed this hard or this well, and I wanted his accolades, yearned for his approval. I had constantly scanned the stands but had not been able to spot him.

Dad worked some Saturdays as a telephone engineer. Since all our games were on Saturday mornings, he missed most of them. But he told me he would be here today, even if he had to quit. If we won this game, we would complete the only undefeated season in the history of that league. So, where was he?

In my mind, an imbroglio of emotions was playing: the elation at having played the game of my life; the bone weariness of a hundred crunching blocks; the disappointment and anger at my dad. How could he have broken his promise and missed this contest?

The gun sounded the end of the game and thoroughly deflated what was left of my hope. As I walked toward the dressing room, I kept asking myself why this meant so much to me. It wasn't just his absence; half the guys never had family members attend the games. It wasn't just that he'd missed my stellar performance; it was the stinging pain of knowing that something had become more important to my dad that morning than me.

In the locker room, the anger mounted when I got my jersey caught on a shoulder pad as I was pulling it over my head. Trying to dislodge it, I ripped it across the back. In a rage, I tore off the shoulder pads and threw them in the direction of the locker.

That's when I realized how quiet the room had become. Everyone else had been enjoying the victory. But not me. My anger stood out like a sore thumb. Our defensive captain, a good friend of mine, ventured a question, "What's wrong, Mike?" All ears were waiting for the answer I couldn't possibly give.

"Tell ya later," I said, hoping to put him off. "It's nothing special." That seemed enough to satisfy the collective curiosity. They all went back to their partying, and I put a lid on my steam. I quickly changed into my old jeans and t-shirt and left the room. I barely acknowledged the congratulations of the coach who commented on my three league records: most converts, longest kick-off and most yardage kick-off total for one game.

I ran down the cement gangway, fighting back tears that confused me as much as they annoyed me. I needed Dad more than I had ever admitted to myself. Walking up the concrete stairs became a chore. But when I reached the outer walkway, I heard a voice call out behind me.

"Wait a minute, superstar—let me buy you lunch!"

It was my dad! He was coming out of the walkway gate. His arms opened wide to embrace me, and I flew to meet him.

"I thought you weren't here, Dad. I looked all over for you."

"I was sitting right behind your bench, down at field level. Didn't you hear me calling out your name?"

Actually, I hadn't heard or seen anything at field level. All my attention had been focused on the grandstand. In a logical, grid-like pattern, I had spent the game scanning the stands. I never thought to look at field level for my dad.

"Quite a passing attack you guys have," my father quipped.

"Yeah, right," I retorted, not letting him go. This was all I ever wanted or needed. He was there as he said he would be.

Commitment. It is the embryo from which fatherhood must grow to girth and maturity. Fathers and their children form a holy circle whose center point is their commitment to one another. And the strongest force in this circle (inevitably the force that binds it together) is the father's stated, implied and fulfilled promises to his children.

My dad was there for that game, but it wasn't long before he left my life forever. He died one month before my seventeenth birthday. At the funeral, I couldn't cry because the pain was embedded so deep, like lava beneath the earth. And it would take four years for the emotion to find a fissure through which to escape. He would no longer be there as he'd promised. He did not live for my forever.

When cancer attacked my father, he would not subject himself to the ignominies of hospital life. He wanted to be at home, sheltered in the comfort of the family he loved. Two-and-a-half months before his death, he finally met Jesus Christ the Lord. That meeting was as tempestuous as his life, and in a moment of faith, he surrendered his soul to the cleansing power of the Savior.

He was transformed that day. Mom read the Bible to him for hours at a time. When he wasn't sedated, he was hearing the Word of God and getting to know the Father he had neglected for forty years. His wilderness experience came first in his life; now he had entered the Promised Land.

Approximately three weeks before he died, he asked me to come in and talk with him. He asked many questions about my plans for the future. Then he stopped and looked me in the eye.

"Mike, please remember something."

"What, Dad?"

"It's not easy to know God. It's much easier not to know Him. It takes work to know God."

"I don't understand."

"Mike, I wasted forty years of my life not knowing God. I've learned a lot in two months because I had to."

He paused, then he said, "Mike, you don't have time to waste. Know God's Son now."

I recall reading a major news magazine when the media was replaying the tragedy of the *Challenger* space shuttle accident. The most disheartening aspect of that scene was the comment made by the son of the flight commander.

The realization of what had happened began to pass over the crowd in a wave of horror. But this small boy stood thinking. As the implications filtered down to the level of his understanding, he began to weep and shudder. Suddenly, he began to call out for his daddy. As his grief mounted he finally cried out with a loud voice, "Daddy, you promised you'd come back—you promised—you said you would!"

His father had broken his commitment to his son, though unintentionally.

Commitment. It is a heavy word, weighted down with cultural anvils and a thousand reasons for guilt. From one perspective, it looks safe, reminding us that we have purpose in life because of our commitments. From the other side, it is a taskmaster, placing us on the rack when we spend hours playing golf instead of reading *The Berenstain Bears and the Moving Day* for the sixty-fifth time that month to our son or daughter.

Commitment. It is slippery in definition, constantly before us, standard as apple pie, felt deeply like spring love and, at times, avoided like the plague.

From *To Be a Father Like the Father* by Michael E. Phillips. ©1992 by Christian Publications, Inc.

Michael Phillips began writing as a teenager in Canada. Mike has been published with *Leadership Magazine*, *Your Church*, *Alliance Life*, *Computing Today* and is the author of *To Be a Father Like the Father*. He currently pastors a pioneer church in Sacramento, California with The Christian and Missionary Alliance. He and his wife, Kathy, have three teenage children.

E-mail: zaphod35@hotmail.com

The Day of Trouble

Agnes Cunningham Lawless

We loved the lakes, the snow-capped mountains and the temperate climate of our Seattle-area home in Bothell, Washington. My husband, John, our son, Ken, and I were happy there for twenty-two years.

Then a letter from an uncle in Maine turned our lives upside down. A few months before, my eighty-six-year-old mother-in-law had fallen and broken her hip while shoveling snow. Now small strokes caused her to fall frequently, but she did not want to go into a nursing home.

"What shall we do?" I asked John.

"Pray and then sleep on it." He held my hand and prayed, "Lord, please show us what to do."

"Beyond a shadow of a doubt," I added.

That night John fell asleep quickly, but I tossed for hours. *Lord, how can we leave our friends and church?* I prayed.

The next morning as I read my Bible, these verses stood out to me: "If a widow has children . . . these

187

should learn first of all to put their religion into practice by caring for their own family and so repaying
their parents . . . for this is pleasing to God. . . . If anyone does not provide for his relatives, and especially
for his immediate family, he has denied the faith and is
worse than an unbeliever" (1 Timothy 5:4, 8).

"John, listen to this," I said. I read the verses to him.

My husband stroked his chin. "I've been thinking
that we should take care of Mother," he said. "After all,
she spent years caring for me when I was growing up."

"True," I agreed, "but won't you lose benefits if you
take early retirement?"

"Yes, but if we're obedient, the Lord will supply
our needs."

That evening we talked the matter over with our
eighteen-year-old son.

Ken was shocked. "But I'll have to leave all my
friends—all the kids I've grown up with!"

John put his arm around Ken's shoulders. "I know
it will be hard for you. At least you'll graduate before
we leave and hopefully we'll be back."

I wasn't so sure. Would my husband want to stay
permanently in Maine where he grew up? His mother
might live for years. I'd always known her to be a lively,
ninety-pound lady who biked five miles a day in good
weather.

We finally decided to sell our home, since we
weren't sure how long we would be gone. Soon
school was out, and we held garage sales, packed and
hired a moving van. I flew on ahead to care for
Mother while John drove the car with our big collie

sitting regally in the back seat. Ken drove his truck out later after finishing a short-term job.

Mother's white colonial-style home with black shutters was typical of New England architecture. After we moved in, Ken got a job, I cooked and did housework and John devoted himself to caring for his mother. Her small strokes increased and she became more incapacitated and short-tempered.

One morning, I set her breakfast on a TV tray. Her short, gray hair curled softly around her face, and she looked like everyone's grandmother as she sat propped up in an overstuffed chair. She slowly stirred her oatmeal, then took a spoonful.

"This is cold!"

"It was hot when I dished it."

"Take it away! I can't eat it." She wiped her mouth and glared at me. "What's wrong with you? Can't you do anything right?"

I carried it back to the kitchen and ran upstairs. Throwing myself on our bed, I wept hot tears of resentment. *Why was she so cruel?*

John walked in and rubbed my shoulders. "What happened?"

I told him and added, "I don't know how long I can stand this. She says such cutting things!"

"Honey, the strokes have affected her personality. She's just not herself."

I pulled a tissue from a box and wiped my eyes. "I know. I'll just have to develop a thick skin."

During our Bible reading together, God spoke to me through a verse: "Call upon me in the day of trouble; I will deliver you, and you will honor me" (Psalm

50:15). We knelt, and I prayed, "Lord, we call upon
you in this day of trouble. Help us . . . and forgive me
for getting upset."

As time passed, John's mother couldn't even lift a
spoon to her mouth or talk. She spelled out her wishes
on an alphabet card.

We began to read the Bible and pray with her every morning, and my attitude gradually changed.
The more helpless she became, the more God's love
and compassion within me grew. I thought how difficult this illness must be for her.

One afternoon, I spoon-fed her, then put my arm
around her and said, "I love you."

Reaching for her alphabet card, she spelled out, "I
love you, too." She gazed at me with a radiant smile,
her blue eyes flooded with tears.

I held her frail hands and thought of the verse that
had meant so much to me months before: *Call upon
me in the day of trouble; I will deliver you.* Yes, that was it.
I had called on God for help, and He had wonderfully
answered.

A few months later, my mother-in-law slipped
away in her sleep—just as she had hoped. How
thankful I was that God had filled me with his love
for this tiny lady, one of his saints.

And I need not have worried about John wanting
to stay in Maine. One winter morning, he took our
collie for a walk. The temperature had plummeted to
35 degrees below zero. A frigid north wind blew so
hard that he had to walk backwards.

When he came inside, he peeled off his jacket, wrapped his arms around himself, and said, "Brrr! Let's go home!"

Agnes Cunningham Lawless is a freelance writer and copy editor in Bellevue, Washington. She has published numerous articles and coauthored four books. She is a graduate of Seattle Pacific University and Prairie Bible College, and did graduate work at Syracuse University, Hartford Seminary Foundation and the University of North Dakota. Agnes taught English and writing at Northwest College and Cascade Bible College, and is currently active in the Northwest Christian Writers Association.

E-mail: agneslaw@aol.com

God's Financial Restoration Program

Ellen Bergh

One morning, as my mother and I were leaving our neighborhood grocery store, I shifted my armload of groceries and casually glanced over at my elderly mother. A sudden tenderness for her filled my heart, and before I knew what words were coming out of my mouth I told her , "God is going to restore to you the years the locusts have eaten in your life."

Mom was old country Irish, and she had taken a dim view of my husband and me coming to Christ in our thirties. Now she looked at me with scorn. "And just how is He going to do all that?" she asked in her lilting brogue.

It was a good question. Mom had worked hard all her life, making low wages in spite of her bright intellect. She had single-parented her two girls and now there were no assets for her old age. I had to admit her future did look bleak. All I could say was I sensed His promise. There was no immediate evidence that my premonition was accurate. In fact, a month later, Mom almost got mugged when she was catching a bus to work in Los Angeles. My husband and I prayed harder than ever for God's protection around her.

It was no wonder Mom was skeptical when I spoke of financial matters. In my marriage, our own finances reminded me of a junkyard with relics of broken dreams and old debts littering the landscape. Instead of passing a fairy wand over it all, God was prompting me to clean it up one clunker problem at a time. Lately, he had me working on reconstructing seven years of overdue tax returns—a task so daunting I shrank from doing it and had to force myself to keep at it.

After daily prayer, I set the kitchen timer to tackle the depressing carnage fifteen minutes at a time, sorting through receipts, pay stubs and what documentation I could find about a tax boondoggle dating to time overseas.

I had helped my husband out of similar situations before we were Christians. *If I fix it again this time, won't it all just happen again?* I wondered bitterly. But I knew we needed to come clean to the Internal Revenue Service in order to stop living in fear of reprisals.

My mother voiced her worry that we might have to do jail time for our crime of tax evasion. A Christian friend who was an accountant looked over my seven years worth of forms with the cover letter of apology, and warned me I was admitting too much liability. Yet I felt God wanted me to tell the whole truth.

The day came when I hand carried the forms to the IRS with my letter of apology. We threw ourselves on the mercy of God and waited for the tidal wave of penalties that could capsize our finances. When the IRS audited the returns, they actually found refunds due some years that offset other penalties we owed. We paid up with an amount far lower than what we expected and we were finally free of the yoke of worry. *Hallelujah!*

When I reported the favorable outcome to Mother she didn't say much. Two months later she called jubilantly and said, "You know, watching you face up to that mess gave me the courage to file for my Social Security. Though I'd paid into it for forty-five years since immigrating from Ireland, I'd doubted whether I was really entitled and never filed for it. Now Social Security has just sent me a retroactive settlement of all I should have collected since I turned sixty-five!"

With her windfall and help from my sister, Mom bought a home in Portland, Oregon. Within a few days of moving in, she inherited a house full of furniture my brother-in-law had in storage since his mother's death. God continued His abundant restoration to Mom and crowned it all with the unexpected blessing of another granddaughter the year she turned seventy-one.

God has been faithful to the message he gave me that day at the grocery store about my mother's future and my own. What God restores is permanent. Years have gone by, and we haven't had to hide from the IRS again. Even my skeptical mother has had to admit God really *does* keep His promises.

Ellen Bergh began writing after graduating from college at age forty-five. She has published inspirational meditations, disability newsletters, personality profiles, book reviews and technical manuals. She founded The Antelope Valley Christian Writers Guild in the high desert area of Southern California.

E-mail: mastermedia@hughes.net

Standing in Lily Lake

Susan M. Warren

"You're not even human!" I cried, anger boiling in my chest.

My mother folded her arms. "I want that car in the garage and you back home by 10:30. We have church in the morning." With that, she stalked back to the kitchen, leaving my teenage wings shredded on the bedroom floor.

I seethed as I watched her go. She had no idea how embarrassing it would be for me to tell my friends that I had to be home by 10:30 on a Saturday night. I was sixteen, not a child! I slouched on the bed, running my hands through my gelled, short-clipped hair. The streak of purple I'd added shortly after the New Year had almost faded. I'd been forbidden to retouch it, another expression of my parental bondage.

How could she do this to me? Didn't she care about my life? She wanted Pollyanna for a daughter—a girl dressed in frills and long blonde braids. But I would never fit into that mold. We were worlds apart, in appearance and goals.

She grew up in a small town, the head cheerleader and the top of her class. She married the class president and wanted to be a nurse and mother. I, on the other hand, barely pulled a 3.0 average, and mocked the cheerleaders in their short skirts and letter sweaters. My "uniforms" were rag-stock army fatigues and bowling shirts obtained from the local army surplus store. As for goals, I thought those were something hockey players shot their pucks into. I knew I embarrassed her. There was no way we would ever find common ground.

The only thing we agreed on was summer camp. Somehow our church's wilderness camp fit into my army-fatigue lifestyle and I'd been an ardent camper from the age of twelve. The camp, located on a small lake in northern Minnesota, encouraged the tomboyish elements that I loved and added a significant dose of the gospel to suit my mother. In truth, the life-challenges of rock climbing, white-water canoeing and backpacking always ignited a spark of religious fervor in my heart. I left wanting to know God better, to serve Him more. Often, during those excursions into faith, I prayed and asked the Lord to help me love my mother.

It was my father who suggested a family canoe trip. Perhaps it was birthed by a desire to grapple with the forces of nature, or maybe he wanted to experience the ultimate family adventure. Whatever the case, we were in over our heads. We planned a trip into the Quetico National Forest in northern Minnesota. It was an uncharted, unkempt area, where beginning canoeists are advised *not* to enter. But Dad figured he had me, and my brother, Dave, who by then was also a wilderness fanatic. With two eager teenagers as guides, what could go wrong? The only liabilities were my ten-year-old sister and my mother, both tentative travelers at best.

A friend towed us by motorboat through Lac La Croix to the entrance of Quetico. I remember vividly his worried expression as we paddled away.

The first night out it poured as if the heavens had overturned a bucket. The sky was pitch dark and we paddled a black lake searching for a campsite. Dad flicked his flashlight over the shoreline, found an indentation and we pulled in. He didn't even bother to hang our food pack, figuring the bears were wiser than we—they knew better than to venture out in that downpour. We ate cold oatmeal for supper.

The next day the sky was as blue as a robin's egg. We paddled eight miles, zigzagging across lakes until we came to a one-mile portage. My mother and sister donned Duluth packs and marched off. I lifted my canoe and followed. My steps were slow and steady—that is, until my father, his voice edged in panic, shouted that he couldn't see my mother up ahead. We almost ran the rest of that portage.

We found my mother perched on a large boulder, sipping water, sporting a glistening layer of sweat and grinning. My dad patted her on the shoulder. I said nothing.

That night, I pulled out my nylon hammock and strung it between two trees. My mother raised her eyebrows. "What about bears?" she asked.

I waved her away and, to my amazement, she shrugged and climbed into her tent. Later that night, as noises howled around me, I joined her—leaving my hammock, and my pride, swaying empty in the wind.

The next day we dropped our entire canister of purification pills in Mirror Lake. My dad pronounced it clean and we filled the water bottles.

We got lost on the fourth day, taking a wrong turn as we bushwhacked through a swamp-like portage. Day five found us ten miles off course, headed in the wrong direction and with only two days left to find the trail and meet our pick-up party. My father and mother studied the map—as if that would help—and I noticed that my mother had taken to wearing a bandana on her head, like a modern-day hippie. Her face was streaked with dirt and her hands calloused. She looked distinctly human, roughed up and real. She smiled at me.

We decided on an intercept course that meandered through unused territory. The trails were overgrown and the lakes filled with bald timber that snagged our canoes. Finally we found the portage that would connect us to Lily Lake, and our preplanned route.

The portage was a scant trail disappearing into a foreboding forest. I watched my mother and sister trot ahead, and the trees swallowed them. As I followed them, a sliver of fear pierced my heart. I plodded along silently, hearing twigs snap beneath my boots and an occasional low-hanging branch squeak as it shuddered along the upturned keel of my canoe. Often I slowed to step over downed trees or to consider where the trail might be turning.

Finally the forest seemed to thin. I spied milky blue between the trees and hustled my pace. Stumbling over a log, I landed knee-deep in a bog of mud. Gritty brown muck crawled its way up my pant legs and around my hips until I was almost waist deep. I imagined tiny mud fleas finding new homes in the pores of my skin, and cried out.

I heard my mother's voice from the other side of the bog. I couldn't see her, because the canoe resting on my head was blocking my vision. I figured I looked like some sort of elongated aluminum mushroom poking up from the earth.

"Throw off the canoe!" she yelled. "We'll pull it through!"

For the first time in ages, I obeyed her on command. I turned the canoe off my shoulders and let it float in the bog. My mother was standing on firm ground at the far edge. She extended a paddle and hooked it around the gunwale of the canoe. I hung on and she pulled me out. She smiled. I thought of my earlier prayer: *Lord, help me love my mother.*

We waded right into Lily Lake, clothes and all, and splashed each other playfully. I saw her tears streak through the mud on her face. They matched my own. We embraced, finally standing on common ground.

Susan M. Warren is a mother of four children, a career missionary with SEND International in Khabarovsk, Russia, and author of numerous devotionals, articles and short stories. She currently publishes a bimonthly newsletter about ministry in Russia, and is completing her first novel.

E-mail: susanwarren@mail.com

A Birthday Surprise

Jennifer Anne Messing

"May I take your order, please?" The voice broke into my thoughts above the din of the busy Portland, Oregon restaurant. December is always such a hectic time of the year. I was relieved that a waitress had finally come. As I turned to face her, I froze. Could it really be my sister Jiji—who lives in the Philippines—taking my order?

"Jiji!" I cried. I stood up and hugged her.

"Happy birthday, Jen," my younger sister answered, flashing a big smile. A few steps behind Jiji came my mother. Another surprise. My husband, two daughters and some close friends had invited me out for dinner. What were Mom and Jiji doing here?

As my Mom embraced me and I heard my friends chuckling and conversing in the background, I realized they had just pulled a big surprise on me. I'd had no idea about Mom's and Jiji's plans to be here for my thirty-first birthday!

An atmosphere of joy and merriment pervaded that evening. Later, however, as the party wound down, a barrage of confusing thoughts filled my mind: Why hadn't my husband been considerate enough to let me know they were coming? How long were they staying? Michael should have known my mom and I had a very strained relationship! Outwardly I smiled; but inside, resentment began to fester.

A busy and somewhat turbulent three-week visit followed, as Mom and Jiji stayed for Christmas and into the new year. We all shopped, baked, planned Christmas day and went to church together. Achieving harmony in our daily schedules became more and more of a challenge. My slow-paced lifestyle clashed with Mom's tireless energy. Tension mounted.

Finally, an angry confrontation erupted between Mom and me. Past hurts were dug up and spewed out. We both said hurtful things to each other. It became so bad that Mom stated, "I'm leaving. Tomorrow I will move in with Michael's mother for the remainder of my stay."

The next morning, following my husband's advice, I forced myself to do something I found very difficult. I walked slowly into my Mom's bedroom, took a deep breath and said softly and deliberately: "Mom, despite our differences, I still love you. I don't want you to leave. I want you to stay."

Tears filled our eyes. Mom looked at me and said, "All right. I am not going to move out, Jennifer. I will stay." Then she walked over and gave me a tight hug. "I do care for you," she added, "though you may not think so. I care for you very much."

That single incident tore down long-standing walls of bitterness and pride between us. My anger and bitterness toward my mother had always prevented me from seeing her good qualities. The forgiveness and unconditional love we extended to each other at that time paved the way for the Lord to do a deeper, purifying work in my heart. He opened my eyes to see many positive qualities about her, qualities that had always been there but which I had never appreciated before: her deep love for God and His people, for instance, as well as her generosity. The Lord softened my heart toward my mom—softened a part that had grown cold and crusty with the years.

On her last day in Portland, Mom treated me to lunch. Guiding my three-year-old daughter through a chaotic buffet line was challenging and tiresome. Then we finally settled down.

"Jen," my mom said, "I just wanted to take you out to lunch to tell you I love you, and I am proud of you. I am thrilled to see what God is doing in your life. You are a very good wife and a caring mother. I see God using you mightily in the worship-leading ministry, and now also more and more in the area of Christian writing. You have matured in the Lord."

My heart warmed as I drank in those affirming words. They were unexpected, yet the Lord only knows how deeply and how long I had yearned to hear them!

Later, when I dropped Mom off at the airport, I cried. It was the first time in my life that I wept when we parted. Wistful regret filled my heart for the years we had lost in our relationship, but I looked forward to a richer and more loving bond between us in the future.

What a wonderful birthday surprise God had prepared for me—a work of healing in my heart! It's never too late for God to restore a wounded family relationship.

> *He will turn the hearts of the [parents] to*
> *their children, and the hearts of the chil-*
> *dren to their [parents]. . . . (Malachi 4:6)*

Jennifer Anne Messing was born in Manila, Philippines and now resides in Oregon with her husband and two daughters. Her articles and poems have been published in several magazines and in the book *More God's Abundance*. She holds diplomas in Journalism and Computer/secretarial, and is Secretary for Oregon Christian Writers.

E-mail: MnJMessing@cs.com

Section 6

Grandparents

*Is not wisdom found among the aged?
Does not long life
bring understanding?
(Job 12:12)*

Red and White Carnations

Barbara Benedict Hibschman

I t was the first Mother's Day since my grandmother passed away. I dreaded going to
church and seeing families sitting together
with their moms. I hated being in church alone, and
today, I hated to admit to myself and others that my
mother had left and my parents were divorced. I
never talked much about it, but later I realized everyone in the church knew more about it than I did.

"Maybe I should have stayed home," I said to myself as I walked up the church steps. A kind elderly
gentleman opened the large wooden door for me.

In the narthex, Mrs. Spence greeted churchgoers.
"Please take a red carnation if your mother is living,
and a white one if she has passed on," she instructed.

I stood in front of the large basket of flowers for
several minutes. I couldn't decide which one to take.

My real *mother is alive, but dead to me*, I reasoned.
She had left when I was two years old, and I had only
seen her twice in all of my sixteen years.

The first time she showed up was two years earlier.
It was my brother's high school graduation. Mrs.

Davis, a teacher, came up to me and said, "Barbara, this is your mother."

"My mother!" I snapped. "What is *she* doing here?"

Behind Mrs. Davis stood a short, brown-haired lady with a warm smile.

"Hi, Barbara," she greeted. "You've turned out to be quite a young lady."

"Hello," I managed to respond. She looked at me and waited for me to say something else. I didn't know what to say or what to do. The seconds seemed like hours. I just stood there and looked at her. *Do I look like her?* I wondered.

Janice, one of my classmates, rescued me from the awkward moment by asking me to meet some friends on the stage to have our pictures taken. I excused myself and made sure I was lost in the crowd.

The second and last time I saw her was at Grandmother's funeral. She tried to talk to me then, but I just looked down. I didn't feel like talking to anyone.

I have a mental image of what she looks like, but no memories of anything we ever did together. To call her Mother seemed strange because it was Grandmother Benedict who was like a real mother to me. She took care of me, went shopping with me and saw to it that my homework got done.

I really should take a white carnation, I rationalized. She was the *real* mother to me. She was there when I needed to talk. She taught me the art of homemaking. She instructed me in cooking and baking—the Hungarian way.

I have fond memories of her sitting by her quilting frame and singing hymns in her native tongue. I would sit and listen to her stories of how she immigrated to America, and how God kept her safe. She told me how God provided her needs. She would always say, "Use what God gives you wisely. If you pray for your daily bread, then don't waste it."

Looking back, I know her faith and the time I spent with her passed on influences that were like the patchwork quilts she made: many fragmented pieces sewn together to form a complete pattern. The dominant pieces were love, joined together by threads of laughter and tears.

I pulled a white carnation from the basket and took a seat in the back pew. The organist began the prelude, and quiet settled over the congregation. I sat clutching the white carnation, while my heart held tightly to the past. Grief surfaced again and I saw nothing promising in my future. Most of the people around me knew that my *real* mother was alive. *Would they understand why I took a white carnation? Does God understand that I'm hurting?*

The choir began to take their seats. The organist played softly. I raised my eyes and focused on the large wooden cross behind the choir loft.

Oh, Jesus, I prayed silently. *You do understand, don't You? You were hurt. You were rejected by those You loved. Yet You chose to forgive them. Help me to do the same. If I meet my mother again, help me to be loving. Thank You that You are always near, and that You promise never to leave me. Thank You for eternal life, and that I will see Grandmother again. Amen.*

The organist continued to play as the pastor took his seat behind the pulpit. I looked back in the narthex and noticed the basket of flowers. Quickly, but quietly, I walked back to the flower arrangement to put the white carnation back. I wanted to prove to God—and myself—that I was willing to deal with the past and the future.

All of the red carnations were taken, but my eye caught a glimpse of one single red and white carnation lying on the table. It probably had been taken out of the basket because it was neither all red nor all white.

"God does understand my feelings!" I said. "The florist didn't make a mistake. This carnation is just right for me on this Mother's Day. I do have a mother who is alive and needs my forgiveness. Grandmother Benedict is gone for now, but alive spiritually and in my memories."

I took the red and white carnation back to my seat and entered into the worship service.

Barbara Benedict Hibschman team teaches at marriage retreats with her pastor-husband, Jim. She is a mother, grandmother, former missionary to the Philippines and teacher. She is the author of eight books and a contributing author to nine devotional books. Barbara is a popular speaker for women's groups and Christian education, missions and writers' conferences. The Hibschmans live in Basking Ridge, New Jersey.

E-mail: 104115.1574@ compuserve.com

What Did You Expect?

Arleta Richardson

My grandmother was a firm believer in prayer. She assured me that God always answered when we prayed in faith. Sometimes He said, "No, not now" or "Wait patiently" and sometimes He said, "Yes" immediately. I never tired of hearing Grandma's stories about God's answers to her prayers.

"Grandma, tell me about the time Grandpa needed shoes."

Grandma would settle back in her chair, rest her crocheting in her lap and we would go back together to a little farm in northern Michigan.

Well, Grandpa and I had moved to the farm. All week he worked hard to make a living for us. Your mother was just a little girl then, and your uncle just a baby. On Sundays, Grandpa preached in the little church at the Corners. None of the people who came had any more money than we did, but they were generous

213

with chickens and fruit and vegetables. We always had lots to eat.

But finally the day came when Grandpa said, "Mabel, I just can't get up in the pulpit again with these shoes. My toes are coming out, and I'm afraid to move for fear someone will see them."

It was true. His toes were out and his mended socks could be seen taking the air. "Well," I said, "we have no money for shoes and nothing to sell to get any. We'll have to ask the Lord for them."

Grandpa did not believe that we should ever ask the Lord for something we could provide if we set our mind to it. But shoes did seem to be out of the question, so we began praying for a pair of shoes. I am sure Grandpa thought about those shoes several times during the week, but he never mentioned them again. He went about his work on the farm, confident that the Lord would provide what was needed.

On Saturday morning, a buggy came up our lane, and Grandpa went out to meet it. It was one of our members with a chicken for Sunday dinner. After chatting for a while, the visitor said, "Oh, by the way, Brother Williams, I bought a pair of shoes last week and they just don't feel right on me. I wonder if you might be able to wear them?"

Grandpa beamed and answered, "Yes, sir, I certainly can!"

The visitor was surprised.

"Why, how do you know?" he asked. "You haven't tried them on yet!" (I would wiggle in anticipation at this point in Grandma's story, for Grandpa's answer was the best part.)

"I'm not worried about that," replied Grandpa. "When the Lord sends me shoes, He sends the right size!"

Grandma would chuckle and resume her crocheting.

"That's the way the Lord treats His children, you know," she would say.

While Grandma's stories thrilled me, and I had a healthy respect for her prayers, it was not until I was nine years old that I was privileged to witness an answer that convinced me that God did indeed listen when Grandma spoke.

We had been making jelly that morning, and the sun shone through the filled glasses on the table. The paraffin to pour on top was heating slowly on the stove. Suddenly, a small spark touched the paraffin, and it blazed up, igniting the wall behind the stove. Quickly the fire spread to the ceiling. Terror-stricken, I began to run toward the door. I shall never forget Grandma as she stood with the wooden spoon in her hand and looked up at the ceiling.

"Lord, please put it out!" she said.

And He did. That very moment. Not a spark was left. Had it not been for the blackened wall and ceiling, I might have thought I dreamed it. I stood wide-eyed and open-mouthed as Grandma began calmly to clean up the mess.

"Well, child, what did you expect?" she asked when she discovered that I still stood speechless in the doorway. "Did you think the Lord would let the house burn down around our ears?"

What had I expected? I will have to admit that had there been time to think about it, I would not have expected a miracle. Oh, yes, I knew God performed miracles. I was brought up on those stories. But for me? That was too much to presume. My first reaction had been to call a neighbor, not God.

Have you seen any miracles lately? You've never seen one? There is only one reason for that: you haven't asked! God doesn't reserve miracles for grandmas or preachers or people who have had a lot of experience in praying. He has them ready for any of His children who call for one.

Remember though, a miracle is not something you could do for yourself. It is an "impossible" in your life. It is a spot with no out. It is for the place where your only foreseeable future is disaster. This is the time to put in an urgent request for a miracle. And this is the time, as surely as you are God's child, that you will see one.

Well, what did you expect? That's the way the Lord treats His children, you know!

Arleta Richardson began her writing career after she had already enjoyed a full career as a college professor, a librarian and an elementary school teacher. Her first book in the now successful ten-book *Grandma's Attic* series was published in 1974. Since then, more than 2 million copies have been sold. More recently, she published the also highly successful *Orphan's Journey* series.

Grandmothers and Tough Love

Dale Evans Rogers
with Carole C. Carlson

One sunny desert day I was driving my daughter-in-law, Linda, two young granddaughters, and a small grandson to a neighboring town for lunch. I had just received a beautiful silver dinner bell from my publisher to commemorate the publishing of *Let Freedom Ring*, my bicentennial book. My gift had been unwrapped and was sitting on the floor of the car.

Enter my grandson, a super-active, bright, inquisitive little guy, who is cute as a button. (Does that sound like a grandmother talking?) D.J. grabbed the bell and began to clang it so loudly that his mother and I couldn't hear each other over the racket. One of his sisters in the backseat reached over to the front and took it from him. He was furious and in a fit of temper, grabbed it and hit her on the head, drawing both blood and tears.

While Linda was soothing the injured one, I firmly took the bell from D.J. and announced, "That's enough! This bell belongs to Grandma, and I will have it quiet!" With that, he threw himself on the floor before the front seat, pushed my right foot on the accelerator, and pressed it to the floor. I kicked his hand off my shoe and with my right hand seized a handful of his hair, giving it a good sharp tug. He yelled like a banshee as I lifted him onto the seat beside me.

Slowing down, I put my arm around him and said, "Honey, I love you, but you cannot behave this way in my car. Your daddy wasn't allowed to do it, and you're not either." He was shocked, to say the least, but soon cooled down.

Perhaps some of you may say, "Why, Dale, surely you didn't pull your grandchild's hair?" Yes, indeed, I did, but he didn't lose any of it. He could have caused a wreck, so it was love, not the devil, that made me do it. He and I are pretty good buddies, although I admit he's so cute I have a temptation to spoil him.

That little story does not imply that I was usurping Linda's right to discipline D.J. Immediate action was needed, action strong enough to leave an impression. Intervention in this case was a necessity, due to the serious consequences of a little boy's temper.

We walk a fine line, grandparents, between loving and overindulgence, between caring and intervention. Our guidelines need to be both common sense (and I love the book of Proverbs for some of the greatest one-liners of all time) and role models of other grandparents.

I had a marvelous role model for my grandmothering years, but I didn't realize at the time that she was establishing the godly principles that I would emulate a generation later. While I was pursuing my intense youthful desires for fame in the entertainment world, Mom was playing surrogate mother to my son, Tom. He called her Mom, and me Frances. She worked hard at not spoiling Tom, and her efforts were rewarded in the evidence of his life.

Promptness is not a virtue bestowed upon us at birth. A child does not have to be taught to be late. One of the rules that my mother had was that dinner was at noon, and everyone had to be in the house, with hands washed, ready to eat when the food was served. This was not a peanut butter and jelly sandwich snack, but a real meat-and-potatoes meal. Tom would wander in after everyone had started to eat, and his grandmother would scold him; however, the next day he would be late again. Finally she said, in that tone so common to exasperated parents, "The next time you're late, I'll teach you a lesson so you won't be late anymore."

Tom was late for dinner again, and this time the punishment was due. Now I'd like to set the stage for the next scene. Imagine a small town in the 1930s. There weren't a lot of exciting events for a young boy, but the high school football games were highlights of his existence. Every high school has its arch rival, and the game of the year was to take place on Friday night. There were banners around town; the tension was high.

My mother called upon her inner resources and said, "Tom, I keep my promises. I told you not to be late again, and you were. You cannot go to the game Friday night."

"Mom," he wailed, "everybody's going to the game. You're not going to make me stay home just for being late for dinner, are you? That's not fair."

How many generations of parents and grandparents have heard the accusation "That's not fair?" It's the national anthem for teenagers.

Well, the days marched toward Friday, with Tom becoming more vocal each hour with his protestations. "Mom, I'll do anything, but please don't make me stay home from the game Friday night. I'll stay home for a month and never be late again. I know you don't want to be so mean."

My mother told me in later years that she never felt so terrible in her life. Other members of the family accused her of being unfair. It was at that point that Mother almost relented.

On the night of the game, Tom went to his room and was heard crying. Mother was in her room, wavering too, because Tom was very precious to her. Afterward she said, "Frances, I believed that if I gave in on that promise, Tom would never respect my discipline again. It was the hardest thing I ever did."

Tom never forgot the lesson. Today he is the most punctual person I know. He's either on time or fifteen minutes early.

Train a child in the way he should go,
and when he is old he will not turn from it.
(Proverbs 22:6)

Excerpted and abridged from *Grandmothers Can*
by Dale Evans Rogers. Copyright © 1985 by
Fleming H. Revell, a division of Baker Book
House. Reprinted by permission.

The late Dale Evans Rogers, actress,
singer, entertainer and best-selling
author was married to cowboy
movie star and singer Roy Rogers,
who died in 1998. She wrote numerous books after her first
best-seller, *Angel Unaware*, published almost fifty years ago. Her
latest book, *Rainbow on a Hard Trail*
is her autobiography—a terrific
bounce back story. On her syndi-
cated television program, *A Date
With Dale*, she shared her faith in
God and her love of America. She
died in February 2001.

It Pays

Stanley C. Baldwin

Shoplifting! Our hearts sank. Our fourteen-year-old son had been caught stealing candy from a local store, and now we had to face the juvenile corrections officer.

We found Skip Hendricks to be a friendly man with an easy manner and a sincere desire to help. However, the action he suggested seemed questionable at the least. It called for us to make an agreement with our son to pay him so much each week *if he didn't steal.*

My initial reaction was negative. *Bribe our son to be good? We are Christians,* I thought. *You don't pay Christians to be good. We are good for nothing.* Despite the humor implicit in the double meaning of that phrase, nothing was funny about our situation. I sensed that our son was at a critical juncture in his life. This could be his first step on a slippery slide into crime and ruin.

Over the next week, we pondered our response to Skip's suggestion. I thought about my principles of child rearing. God gave kids parents because kids cannot foresee the consequences of their actions. Tell a three-year-old to stay away from the street or he might get run over, and it may or may not register. Discipline him—provide immediate consequences for playing in the street—and he will get the message.

Parents are to teach their kids about the real world. If in the real world a behavior will have sad consequences, a parent's job is to make it have sad consequences here and now in a way the child understands.

Good behavior has consequences as well. Our job as parents is to reward good behavior, to reinforce in our children the true belief that *it pays to be good.*

If indeed it pays to be good, why not reinforce that truth right now in a tangible way our son would appreciate? We decided to pay our son not to steal. To our knowledge he never stole again. Today he is a trial attorney and partner in a major law firm.

When our grandchildren entered their teen years, we were concerned about the possibility of their using drugs. What could we do to help them avoid forming substance abuse habits that could mar their lives or utterly destroy them?

We wrote each one a letter at the beginning of the school year. If they finished the year without using drugs, tobacco or alcohol, we would give them $100 to use as they chose. We explained in the letter that we were sure the advantages of not using these substances would prove to be worth a lot more to them than the $100, but we wanted this money to provide a little added incentive right here and now.

How did it work? It is difficult and probably impossible to know how much effect this or any other single measure had. At year's end, one of our grandchildren did not qualify for the $100. Three of them did.

One who did said, "No way would I have used drugs, tobacco or alcohol anyhow, but I appreciate the gift."

The parents appreciated it too. One of them sent a card warmly thanking us for supporting their own child-rearing efforts.

The grandchild who did not qualify for the $100? He gave his parents many concerns for a while, and unfortunately acquired a smoking habit. But then he turned his life around and made us all proud. In a letter thanking me for my input into his life, he said, "Thank you for leaving me a path even a blind man could follow."

Often children *are* blind to the consequences of their actions, good or bad. God helps us to leave clear paths for them to follow. Sometimes that may involve making real to them the consequences of their behavior with rewards as well as punishment.

Stanley C. Baldwin is an internationally known author and speaker based in the Pacific Northwest. A former book and periodical editor, he is author and/or coauthor of twenty books, including four titles that have sold over 250,000 copies. They are *The Kink and I, Your Money Matters, What Did Jesus Say About That?* and *Love, Acceptance and Forgiveness*. Most of his books deal with applying Bible principles to daily life. His books have been translated into eleven languages. Stan has lectured in many countries around the world and he speaks at writer's conferences all across the U.S. He has been director of International Christian Writers since 1996.

E-mail: SCBaldwin@juno.com

Grandpa and Me

Jordan, Age 9

The dad in my life isn't really my dad; he's my grandpa. But he's been like a dad to me since before I was born.

Four months before I was born my real father left my mommy. My grandpa drove 400 miles to come get my mommy and me. He took care of my mommy until I was born. When I came home from the hospital there was a cradle that Grandpa made just for me. Someday, my kids will sleep in the same cradle.

When I was a baby I cried a lot at night. Grandpa would walk me around and around the kitchen table. He rocked me to sleep and he was my first baby-sitter.

Now I'm nine years old and Grandpa is my best buddy. We do lots of things together. We go to zoos, museums and parks. We watch baseball games on TV—just the two of us.

When I was four my grandpa spent a whole summer building me a playhouse with a big sandbox underneath. He made me a tire swing and pushed me lots of times in it. He pushed me real high, way up over his head. Now he spends all his extra time building new rooms on our house so that Mommy and I will have our own apartment. If we didn't live at Grandpa's house we would have to live in a little apartment in town and I couldn't have my dog, my two house cats, my barn cats and my gerbils. My grandpa doesn't like cats very much but he lets me keep two cats in the house and he buys lots of cat food and feeds the barn cats even when it's really cold outside.

My grandpa is really patient. When he is busy building things he always takes time to start a nail so that I can pound it in. After he's spent all day mowing our big lawn he is really tired, but he will still hook my wagon up to the lawn mower and drive me all over the place.

My grandpa loves Jesus and he wants me to learn about Him too. Sometimes people on TV talk about kids from single-parent families. I'm not one of them because I have three parents in my family. My grandpa isn't my father, but I wouldn't trade him for all the dads in the world.

> Submitted by Jordan, age 9, to the National Center for Fathering's Father of the Year Essay Contest. Used by permission. For information call 1-800-593-3237 or visit www.fathers.com.

Treasure from Grandma

Betty Southard

*I*f you were lucky enough to know one or both of your grandmothers, you may well have special treasures from her. Oh, I don't mean money or jewelry or antique furniture, although some of you may have that as well. The treasure I'm thinking of is far more precious, and its value is reserved just for you. Pam McComb-Podmostko wrote of such a treasure.

Pam's grandmother's most prized possession was a five-by-seven portrait of Grandpa that she kept in a frame on her dresser for more than fifty years. Each time Grandma walked past her dresser she motioned her hand as if to wave, and she would say "hi" to "my Bob." Grandma wouldn't have given that photo up for a million dollars.

Since Pam lived in another state, she wasn't able to visit her grandmother very often, but every time she did, Grandma gave her a box of "treasures" to open when she got home. Although the treasures weren't worth much in dollars and cents, they were always precious to Pam, for in them she saw Grandma sharing something of herself.

After an especially enjoyable visit when Pam and Grandma worked together on an oral family history, Grandma said good-bye and, as usual, handed Pam a box of treasures to open when she got home. There were the usual things—little dishes, old family letters and the like. But when Pam got to the bottom of the box, she noticed something very carefully wrapped in tissue paper and tied with a ribbon. Gently she untied it to find Grandma's greatest treasure in all the world—the portrait of Grandpa that had stood for all those years on Grandma's dresser.

"I was proud and honored that Grandma would give her most prized possession to me," Pam wrote. "Then suddenly I felt terribly afraid. There could only be one reason she parted with it. She must have known her time on this earth was growing short."

A few months later, Pam's grandmother had a stroke. Although Pam had been told it wouldn't be worth the expense of the airplane trip to visit her comatose grandmother, she packed her bag and went anyway. Carefully Pam tucked "Grandma's Bob" in her suitcase. She knew if anything would get a response, it would be that picture.

Pam was not prepared for the woman she found on the bed in her grandma's hospital room. She took Grandma's thin hand, rubbed it and talked to her. No response. Pam begged Grandma to open her eyes and look at what she had brought. No response.

Pam didn't give up. Again and again and again she tried to rouse Grandma. Three days later, Pam saw

Grandma struggle to open her eyes. "It was only momentarily but I showed her the photo of her Bob," Pam said. "She looked at it, then her eyes met mine. Our hearts touched and once again her eyes closed. A single tear rolled down her cheek."

Pam's grandmother never opened her eyes again. She died quietly two months later.

Is Pam McComb-Podmostko a wealthy lady? You bet she is! Her grandmother left her a priceless treasure of shared love.

What are you doing to put away a treasure for your grandchildren? Are you storing away memories of unconditional love, understanding and acceptance? Are you making consistent investments of time and attention with your grandchildren? Are you using your gifts to individually build up each one of them?

Give yourself permission to enjoy the name and role of grandparent. Rejoice in who you are and take joy in each of your grandchildren too. You say you want to boast and brag on them? Great! Do it! Grandparents are expected to see their grandchildren as the most perfect, beautiful, smart and talented children in the world. So go ahead and brag. Pull out the pictures. Tell the cute stories and repeat the clever sayings. It's your right as a grandparent. As one of the ladies in our grandmothers' group said so eloquently, "We grammies are special people. We love, we care, we are there."

Yes, we are and yes, we do!

Betty Southard is a dynamic communicator who lives and teaches God's Word. Betty is a teacher for Christian Leaders, Authors, and Speakers Seminars (CLASS), and an adjunct professor at Biola University and Minister of Caring for the Hour of Power International Ministry. Along with many articles, she has authored two books, *The Grandmother Book* and *Come As You Are*.

E-mail: BettySCA@aol.com

Get Back on the Horse

Monica Johnson

The sun was warm on our backs as we saddled up the horses. The smell of the dairy cows was in the air. I pushed back my cowgirl hat, trembling with excitement.

I had been riding high in the saddle with my grandfather ever since I was big enough to grab on to a saddle horn. Riding a horse was just about my favorite thing in the world to do. But today was extra special. Today was my big day. Today, I was six years old and grandpa was going to let me sit in the saddle by myself and ride the horse alone.

Spook was a greyish-white gelding with an easygoing disposition and a bit of a stubborn streak. He was always gentle with me, but liked to tease and act kind of sassy with Grandpa. I watched Grandpa's expert hands as he put the bit in Spook's mouth and patted him on the shoulder.

Grandpa's face looked rough and kind at the same time. His whiskers scratched my cheek, but his smile warmed my heart. He always wore blue jeans, a western shirt and a big cowboy hat. He was tall—he looked like a giant to me. He adjusted the reins.

"Ready?" he asked, reaching down to pick me up.

"Ready!" I answered, stretching out my arms to him.

Wow! I never realized Spook was so big. It felt like I was sitting up on top of the barn.

Grandpa saw that my feet didn't quite reach the stirrups. He fixed the right one up and moved around Spook to fix the stirrup on the left. Spook had been standing patiently, swishing his tail to chase away the flies. One must have bit him though, because, in the short time it took Grandpa to walk around him, he gave a twitch, a shake and a shudder.

Boom! There I was on the ground!

My feelings were bruised more than I was, but I let out a howl anyway. Grandpa dried my tears, dusted me off and started to lift me back into the saddle. I pulled away. I was *not* getting back on that horse. No way! I was sure if I did, I would just fall off again.

Grandpa leaned over and looked me sternly in the eye. The words he spoke have stayed with me all my life.

"If you fall off a horse, ya gotta get right back in the saddle. You can't never just give up and walk away. Now, no more cryin'. Just get up and get back on the horse." Not only did I get back on the horse and learn to ride alone that day, I've been following that advice ever since.

My mom, my younger sister, Alicia, and I had recently moved in with my grandparents on their Black Angus ranch in Gilroy, California. I learned early that ranch life involves more than just bouncing up and down on a saddle. Grandpa taught me to feed and curry the horses and how to clean out the stalls. Grandma showed me how to cook the kind of hearty meals that hardworking ranch hands love.

Throughout my growing-up years, my grandparents were always the one dependable constant in my life—my rock of Gibraltar. They were never negative; they always had faith in me. Whenever my world fell apart and my situation was scary, I recalled my grandpa's words. I didn't give up. I "quit crying, dusted myself off and got back up on the horse," so to speak.

A few years ago, Grandpa had to listen to his own advice. Over a period of a few years, he suffered three strokes. The third one was hardest on him. He lost control of his speech and the motor functions on his left side.

This invincible man, as strong as Hercules, now needed help doing almost everything. I knew the strain of this was rough and I almost dreaded the trip to visit them. I was afraid Grandpa would be different. This happened right about the time I became a Christian, so even though I never said the words to them person-ally, I prayed daily for both my grandparents as they faced this challenge. I asked the Lord to give them both the strength to "get back on the horse."

Well, the journey hasn't been without its struggles and stumbles, but today my grandfather is able to do most of the things he likes. I believe his sense of hu-mor and his determination have tripled! He has been my inspiration to acquire those qualities for myself.

When I became a Christian, I realized that the love my grandparents have always had for me was truly heaven-sent. I am thankful for the unconditional love they have given me, just as I am now thankful for the unconditional love that Jesus gives. My faith in God and the memory of my grandfather's advice keep me hanging on to that saddle horn through the unexpected falls and bumps life often brings.

Monica Johnson lives in Boise, Idaho and is in her second year as a member of AmeriCorps, working part-time in a child/parent literacy program. She also attends classes at Boise State University and hopes to become a counselor for teenagers. She loves writing, reading and going camping with her husband and their four young children.

E-mail: learnlab@micron.net

Other books in the *Bounce Back* series
Edited and compiled by Diana L. James
Published by Horizon Books

Bounce Back - 1997
You Can Bounce Back Too - 1998
Teens Can Bounce Back - 1999